Stalking Western Trout

D1601828

Stalking Western Trout
Neale Streeks

Frank
Amato
PORTLAND

Photography: Neale Streeks (unless otherwise noted)
Design: Jerry Hutchinson

ISBN: 1-57188-207-3

© 2001 Frank Amato Publications, Inc.
P.O. Box 82112, Portland, Oregon 97282
(503) 653-8108
Printed in Singapore
1 3 5 7 9 10 8 6 4 2

Table of Contents

Introduction

A trout-stalker looks through the willows and finds a nice rainbow making "head rises" to Trico spinners.

Circles on the water, slow heaves, or brisk splashes interrupting a wandering flow; swallows wheel and dive above, mayflies clumsily unfold their wings, a bit dazed in their brilliant new world...these images have piqued the interest of fishermen from time beyond memory. While the origins of fly fishing are shrouded in history, a continuous written record has been followed since 1496, and perhaps earlier.

Casting to sighted fish and matching the hatch were already intrinsic aspects of the sport at that early date. Twelve fly patterns were suggested, each based on a hatch and time of year. Stomach autopsies were promoted, with flies tied to match what was found within. Over 500 years later, with satellites orbiting overhead and graphite stick in hand, little else has changed.

There have been some distractions. Fishing "blind" with attractor dries and streamers, and strike-indicator nymphing have proven to be excellent fish-catching alternatives, to the point that many modern "got to have it now" anglers don't even bother looking around for fish. On goes the beadhead nymph and indicator, with Gore-Tex-enveloped legs plunging headlong into the trout's feeding flats. When guiding, it's not uncommon to see 7 out of every 10 boats strike-indicator nymphing, even when rising fish are at hand. It's hard to see risers when staring at the bobber and some rowers don't want to interrupt the bobber routine. Nymphing up fish for beginners is a good idea too, since rising trout are easier to spook with errant casts. But for those that look, that know the shallow ways of their quarry, and who are intoxicated by sight-fishing challenges, there is little to match the thrill of "trout hunting" with the dry fly.

Rivers across the West, some famous, others reveling in their obscurity, offer sight-fishing excitement almost year 'round. Between dam-controlled rivers, spring creeks, freestone streams, and lakes, there is usually a playing field to be found within a day's drive. Wipe off your Polaroids, don your hat, and get ready to prowl the banks!

Chapter 1
The Trout's Shallow-Water World

A rainbow turns to the side to intercept a morning Trico spinner.

The serious angler is always keen to witness the life habits of a river valley's inhabitants, be it bird, mammal, fly, or fish. With years of observation, connections are revealed. Raccoons flip rocks to find emerging stonefly nymphs. Migratory birds arrive in sync with the first dense mayfly hatches. Trout lie under choppy riffles to hide from the eyes of osprey and kingfisher.

The trout of course plays the leading role, at least from our point of view. They are lively characters, darting in and out of our sight and approachability. What has made them so desirable for so many centuries are their shallow-water habits. The rings of rising trout push right up against shallow banks. Their graceful spotted forms can be seen gliding, darting, and grubbing off the edges of main and secondary currents. Seeing them "tip up" is the true charm. All can be in plain view, for those that take the time to look. This is the draw.

Bright sunshine backlights swaying willow leaves. Piercing sunbeams cleave between the limbs' shadows, illuminating a golden cobblestone glide. The rings and shapes of trout, fluttering of insects, and circling of swallows brings this valley scene brilliantly alive. An angler can hardly contain his enthusiasm!

Trout are shallow-water creatures to a large extent. Sure, there are big ones lounging in the deepest river depths, and those looking for the comfort of a deep summer run or spring hole, but on the whole, trout are peripheral creatures. They hang about the edges of things; to the sides of heavy currents; at the heads and tails of pools; to the left or right of schools of pool belly whitefish; and along the banks and boulders that confine their watery world. One should never oversimplify an animal's behavior, but from a sporting aspect, this is especially true.

The fact that trout, and especially rising trout, like shallow water is the backbone of our sport. It has been witnessed in thousands of ways, shapes, and forms for hundreds of years. Water as shallow as four inches can and will hold the largest of rising trout, typically topping out at about 23 inches in length. Trout much bigger than that often quit rising altogether (except in places like New Zealand and at night) and with the odd exception, become subsurface feeders, praying on crayfish, sculpin, nymphs, and minnows. Trout of 13 to 23 inches are good sport in anyone's book though, especially when seen "nose up" in some flotsam-dotted bankside glide. These are the ones with which we will be most concerned.

Shallow water has great appeal to trout for several reasons, and over the millennia has become their landlocked domain. (Trout are

Mayfly spinners pile up along banks on summer days. Wind can concentrate them even more. Add some terrestrial insects and you have a nice stew for edgewater trout. Shallow-water zones produce much of a trout's food.

various nymph species—the trout's main food. Other aquatic insects, including stoneflies and some mayflies and caddis, migrate to shallower edgewaters before hatching. The stoneflies crawl out, mostly at night, to emerge. Mayflies, including some *Heptagenia* and *Paraleptophlebia* species, and certain caddis types migrate to the bank side of heavier currents before emerging as winged adults. Warmth-loving minnows ply the shallowest of edgewaters, while damselflies, grasshoppers, beetles, and ants frequently take spills into swirling bankside flows.

Dense hatches and spinner falls also pile up in the slower waters and make easy targets in shallow flats, eddies, and tailouts. Trout can rise or nymph with both the ceiling and the floor within easy reach. Wind will concentrate food along banks, sometimes to a great extent, while often leaving a narrow wind-free slick piled with fly. Trout can rise heartily here. Be alert! For above everything else, what bigger trout want in life is a current-sheltered lie with plenty of food delivered and safety nearby. A moderately shallow edgewater with either protective cover or a deeper or snarled escape route fits this bill.

There are more reasons trout like the shallows. Shade, for instance, draws trout in. They aren't fond of brilliant sunlight, especially when easy options are close by. Trees, shrubs, and even grass can throw enough shadow for a trout to call the area home. They'll move with the shadows as the sun arcs across the summer sky. Shade might be the only place you find risers on a hot summer's day. Other low-light options include deep water and riffles overhead.

thought to have once been all anadromous or sea-run fish that over glaciated periods became landlocked.) One of the main draws of the shallows is the abundance of food to be procured there. Aquatic life diversity and numbers can be greatest in the shallows, in water of under five feet in depth. Sunlight triggers the growth of aquatic plants, algae, plankton, and consequently, insects, crustaceans, and fish. Shallower runs and riffles can support tremendous numbers of

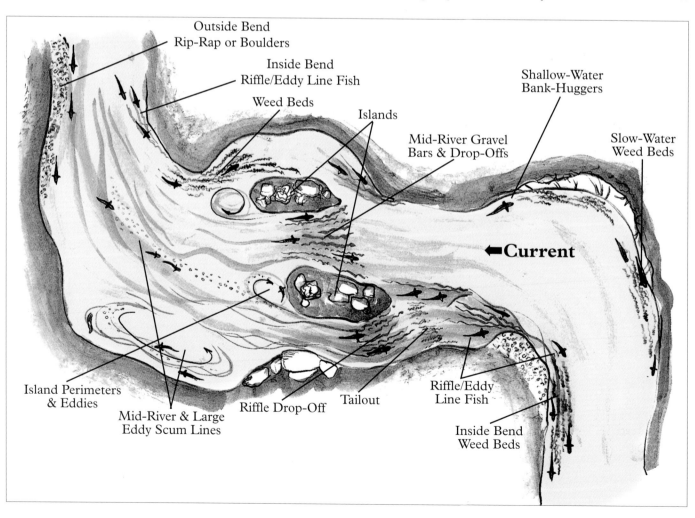

Outside Bend
Rip-Rap or Boulders

Inside Bend
Riffle/Eddy Line Fish

Weed Beds

Islands

Shallow-Water
Bank-Huggers

Mid-River Gravel
Bars & Drop-Offs

Slow-Water
Weed Beds

◄**Current**

Island Perimeters
& Eddies

Mid-River & Large
Eddy Scum Lines

Riffle Drop-Off

Tailout

Riffle/Eddy
Line Fish

Inside Bend
Weed Beds

Some quite large trout will hold in sun-beaten riffle lines, in water as shallow as four inches. The broken surface of a riffle offers camouflage from airborne predators. I've caught numerous browns up to and over 20 inches in such water. They seem more camouflage conscious than rainbows, who will fin openly in flat water, and seem to depend more on their speed.

There is a price to pay for dwelling in the shallows—sharp-beaked birds and high-strung mammals. Trout must be keenly on guard to reach the ripe old age of 3 to 7 years. Kingfishers, blue heron, osprey, cormorant, mergansers, and eagles all relentlessly hunt local waters. Their patience, agility, and eyesight often win them the day. Mink and otter also take their toll, with hot-blooded determination and the hunter's skill. Another natural predator of the trout is man, whose unchecked and spiraling population has shown the ability to eliminate trout by destroying the entire habitat.

Shallow-water trout are edgy creatures indeed, darting from the shadows of birds or the overhead movement of a fly line. Such fish offer the most alluring of sport, but are also quickest to take exception to poorly cast or chosen flies (or even to good ones!). The trout-stalker must be patient enough to observe without being seen, and stealthy enough to fool his shallow-water prey.

It's common to see beginners approach a river in a rush. Not a second is spent looking for actively (or semi-actively) feeding fish, let alone the minutes often needed to successfully scan nearby

Remember that trout are wild animals. Sneak up to banks, camouflaging your silhouette, and look near and far for evidence of resident trout. Some of the largest rising fish are found in the slowest, shallowest waters.

This 22-inch brown was steadily rising to spent caddis on a late July morning. He was holding close to the bank, in just inches of water, pushing big wakes with each rise. Such sight-fishing victories linger in the memory a good long time.

waters, upstream and down, close and far, atop and beneath the surface, for evidence of the best sport. The beginner wades right through productive trout flats, never seeing the V wakes running from his awful presence. He wades knee-deep and begins casting to mid-stream, never experiencing some of trout-fishing's best and most memorable shallow-water action. He should never forget that many of the largest steady-rising fish feed in the slowest and shallowest edgewaters.

Shallow-water, feed-lane, and rising or visible trout are not confined to edgewaters. Mid-stream gravel bars, boulders, logjams, and even slow-water foam lanes snaking across deep pools can provide sight-fishing thrills. Extensive gravel bars, weedbed breaks, and eddy lines that swing out to mid-river, can all be home to numerous rising fish. Trout can sometimes be spotted beneath the water nymphing if the sun is high in the sky. A good hatch will show them grazing the surface, pushed up into mini channels or eddy lines for "first dibs," or dropped back into a converging current lane or flats where a slow but heavily fly-laden foam trail makes the pickings easy. These could be wade-fishing targets on smaller waters, or boat access challenges on big rivers. Wherever they might be found, keep your eyes and mind alert for prime feeding scenarios and the rings of rising fish.

Where river currents slow to a snail's pace (trout love snails too), a different behavior pattern begins to show. Fish begin to cruise and wander, not content with a slower current's provisioning. This goes for some flats and inside bends of rivers, and even more so for big eddies and spring-fed sloughs (not to mention lakes). Most trout will have a personal territory and cruising path or "beat" along which they frequent. It's best to study their beat for a while, and then lead them with your fly by a considerable distance, letting the fish come to it. Here the stalker's patience can pay dividends in sight-fishing success. Trout in four inches to four feet of water might be seen nymphing, rising, or both. It's flat water though and these trout can see well. They're extra edgy and keenly alert to motion and shadow, the signs of death-dealing predators. Long, light tippets and realistic patterns might be needed to win the day, along with a patient timing of casts designed to intercept the fish, not attack it. A bit of wind chop can certainly help mask your duplicity.

A nice eddy-cruising brown inspects a beetle before eating it. We caught him later! This illustrates a classic inspection/head rise/left over bubble-rising sequence. It was a lucky bit of photography.

Now should a dense hatch or spinner fall cover the same slow-water inside bend, trout may then hold a position and rise, though some may cruise and sip eagerly, as they do in lakes, big eddies, and sloughs. Each trout has its own personality. You can never pigeonhole their behavior patterns without being surprised. Spooking unlooked-for trout is definitely part of the stalking game.

There are certainly times of the day and year, and various fish, that find the shallows less inviting. The cold of winter and extreme heat of summer find many fish seeking the shelter of deeper water. In winter, slower water can appeal to trout, whose metabolism and rate of digestion are lowered by cold water. Heated summer water can find them seeking cool sanctuary and the added oxygen of swift deep runs or spring holes. In both cases, this can take fish out of the sight-fishing arena (though the flashes and shadows of nymphing trout can still be seen at times). No matter, here's where indicator nymphing takes the day.

Low light levels (whether caused by clouds, wind, dawn, or dusk) and a lack of hatches limit sight-fishing too. There's nothing like the bold take of a Woolly Bugger in such conditions to keep you going. And while stripping it in, you can still hunt for trout noses. Though many of the fish may be out of sight, it's rare that they all are. There are usually some shallow or slow-water fish that continue to rise, if only occasionally, even in adverse conditions (many trout don't like rising in the wind for instance). Foam-specked eddies may show the odd snout. The inner edge of an eddy line might reveal the occasional spreading ring. The key is to keep your eyes and mind ever alert to the possibilities, to constantly scan the river for likely trout scenarios, staring at each locale in lengthy turn. This is easier to do by not casting till fish are found. If you must cast, streamer fishing leaves your eyes largely free to roam the watery world. Even when hypnotized by the magic bobber, when strike indicator nymphing is paying its substantial rewards, a close look at eddies and such may show a more visual form of sport—which is easily and often overlooked when playing the nymphing game.

These and other aspects of trout-stalking and fish behavior will be investigated in the pages that follow. It's a style of fishing that draws you deeper into the river world, giving you the time and clues to discern its many secrets. Those inflicted with a trout-stalker's mindset no longer just stroll to the river and cast. They prowl the banks, with an ever-growing understanding of the trout's habits and world. He stares, searches, and waits for the telltale signs of fish, and is often rewarded with sights, memories, and fishing opportunities that others never see. Such visual stalking memories linger many days or years—one of the true rewards for the human brain.

There are days when more fish are caught by sight-fishing. These are offset by days when the workmanlike application of deep nymphing easily wins the day. Combining all styles is best, as far as the catching goes. While it's true that only a small percentage of fishermen are ever fated to become pure "trout-stalkers," even traveling the world in search of golden sight-fishing moments, all fishermen will gain pleasure and added success by polishing their trout-stalking skills.

Chapter 2
How & Where To Look For Trout

Geared up and ready to go. Miles of river might be covered, but at a snail's pace. Careful study of the streambed for the wavering shapes of trout takes time. Here, the undercut bank and quieter edgewaters are an ideal zone to find nymphing or rising trout.

The earnest trout-stalker needs no additional equipment to ply his art, he just uses what he has in a more efficient and cunning way. Highly important are the hat (dark-hued under the brim is best) and polarized sunglasses. Side shields for the sunglasses add further viewing enhancement, keeping glaring light off the eyes and inside of the lenses. These are tools most fishermen already have. Some even carry binoculars, to spot distant risers, and to spy on the successes of others. No doubt night spotting scopes have come into play among the most fervent, look for big heads on past twilight.

Clothes should be drab, somewhat camouflaged, and functional. Waders, when needed, should allow a long, yet comfortable hunt. Gore-Tex is a great improvement here, worn with light-weight, sturdy wading shoes. Insulate beneath as needed, even carrying an extra pair of light pile or quilted pants in a daypack. Walking all day in heavy neoprenes has about killed lesser men (myself included). Never has a truck been a more welcome sight than after stumbling the last miles of a day-long jaunt in bootfoots!

A daypack with lunch, water, sunscreen, rain and fishing gear, flashlight, and such keeps comforts and necessities at hand. Pack light to minimize shoulder strain, otherwise you'll feel it by the end of the day. I know. Insect-catching net, stomach pump, a small white bowl to inspect stomach contents, and a camera with various lenses might also be desired by the fanatical. I like to catalog hatches, trout food (from stomach pumping), fish behavior, river scenes, and the occasional big fish on film. I prefer Kodachrome 200 slide film for its greater latitude with close-ups, action shots, and low light conditions. It has beautiful, realistic color tones too. I might add that when shooting film around water glare, you often need to over expose shots by one or more stops. Bracket good shots to be sure. When photographing stomach contents in a white bowl, you need to over expose by 2 3/4 stops! Experiment with your equipment and take notes.

Streamer Fishing

CORRECT

When fishing streamers, use a stout leader and retrieve your fly with your rod tip near the water. Strikes are more easily detected this way and you are in an ideal position to set the hook.

INCORRECT

Poor hook-setting position.

Sagging line makes it harder to detect strikes and set the hook.

Don't retrieve your streamer with the rod tip held high, or use the rod tip to impart all the action to your streamer. It's harder to detect strikes and set the hook.

Boat fishing allows the use of several pre-rigged rods—dry fly, nymph, and streamer. This is a great benefit. Whenever some tantalizing scenario unfolds, you can switch rods to meet the challenge rather than doing a complete re-rig. Besides risers, you can sometimes see fish visibly nymphing. Occasionally you see big V wakes, trout slashing around after baitfish. Being ready to immediately toss

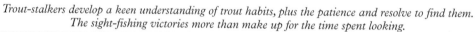

Trout-stalkers develop a keen understanding of trout habits, plus the patience and resolve to find them.
The sight-fishing victories more than make up for the time spent looking.

a streamer in the vicinity has produced some aggressive fish for me and my guided fishermen.

I prefer to go float fishing with only two people aboard, one fisherman and a rower. This allows the back end of the boat to be kept light for better rowing. It can then be used as a rod caddy, holding excess gear and prestrung rods. With only one angler in the front of the boat, and a skilled rower in complete control, trout-stalking afloat becomes a super effective technique (see Chapter 5).

The trick to finding the most rising fish is to constantly look for them. This sounds easy enough, but keeping that concentration level all day is something that many anglers have trouble doing. A slow period finds their interest waning, subtle risers start getting overlooked. Just when you need to be searching the hardest—when the fewest fish are active—is when many let their guard down completely.

Eye strain is also a factor. Consciously staring and searching for the rings and noses of rising trout is more fatiguing than you might think. Some can do it from dawn to dusk. Others tire after just a few hours. In such cases, blind-fishing a Woolly Bugger can maximize your catching chances while you rest your eyes (and the trout of the day might also engulf your Bugger!). Letting them flit about the valley scenery also gives eyes a good break. You can go back to stalking when your eyes are rested, or when hatch activity picks up.

When walking and wade-fishing up a river or stream, think of yourself as a predator. You don't want to brazenly stroll along the banks in plain sight. Stay back a bit, move slowly, minimize your silhouette and shadows. Don't let the fish see you. Any shallow bank could house the largest riser of the day. Trout are wild animals, ever on the alert. Sushi isn't limited to human consumption. Birds and quick movement make them most twitchy. The fish would like to live long and grow fat.

Trout will fin in extremely shallow water when undisturbed, sipping duns, spinners, and terrestrials at their cautious leisure. When first approaching the river for the day, sneak slowly, staying back a bit for a long look. After searching the closest edgewaters, look further up and downstream, and lastly, look across the breadth of the river. Expansive eddy lines or mid-river breaks and gravel bars could show fish. This all takes a little time, so don't rush it. Don't be overeager to get your legs and fly wet.

If there are other fishermen about and no fish are rising, you have several options. You could just keep walking, looking, and being resolved to only casting to sighted fish. Rising, nymphing, cruising, and holding trout might all be visually located. You can search harder than anyone else, looking into every quarter and water type along the way. This can teach you a lot about a river and its fish. Few anglers take this route these days, especially among beginners and those with time constraints. Many are just too eager to not immediately cast. For most anglers, the end result—fish in the net—is the overriding desire. This is understandable.

The purist trout-stalker tends to be very experienced, with plenty of time and enough fish under their belt to have dulled the need for instant action. What he desires instead is one of those premiere sight-fishing experiences with rising, nymphing, or cruising fish, another visual adventure to be locked into the memory banks, as well as into the net.

There are many rising trout that aren't so easy to see. Proximity and background lighting are important factors in finding those hidden fish. Here, a trout uses a floating weed mat for overhead cover, but comes out routinely to rise. His riseform can be difficult to see in the streambank reflections. A different viewing angle could make him stand out more clearly.

Option two, and one I often pursue whether on foot or by boat, is to cast Woolly Buggers, crayfish patterns, and such while progressing slowly and looking for risers or easy-to-see subsurface fish. While the act of fishing dulls your stalking senses to some degree, enough are left to find rising trout. (This is not nearly as true when indicator nymphing, since you hate to take your eyes off that bobber!) You're less likely to spot cruising, nymphing, or holding trout, especially when wade fishing and down in the water. Boat fishing puts you higher up where your visibility is better, much like stalking from an elevated bank. Since you don't need your eyes to retrieve a streamer, you're still in a good position to spot rising or bulging trout. Even trout flashing in a run, twisting to snub a nymph, might be seen. If the light is right, subsurface fish may show themselves here and there. On the whole though, I streamer-fish and hunt risers.

The third choice would be to largely ignore sight-fishing, and fish indicator nymphs, attractor dries, two-fly rigs, or streamers. If a good hatch comes off, you can then return to sight-fishing. Many days this could be the most productive route. An attractor dry fly with a nymph dropper is a great combination on swifter rivers and streams. Fishing the water produces fish and hones casting skills that are useful later for sighted fish. Each river will have its own

Trout are usually easier to see when you're looking upstream, rather than down or across. The way their head pushes and interrupts the flow works in the stalking angler's favor, especially in choppy water and poor light.

character and fishing demands. Spring creeks and some dam-controlled rivers feature slower water, small but abundant insects, and pickier, angler-wary fish. Swift high-country rivers tend to have larger insect types and, often, more aggressive fish. These facts of river life will eventually prove themselves in your fishing experiences and adaptations.

While some trout are easy to see, finning out in wide open waters, especially during dense hatches, others require a greater degree of concentration. Anyone will see fish boiling when bugs are thick. Fewer will see the remaining noses when the hatch or spent wings are all but gone. As the last bugs trickle down banks, bouncing and spinning off blades of grass, or making slow circulations around soupy food-filled eddies, there the hidden fish will be found. Tucked in along a drooping willow bough, lost among jumbled rocks, in the shade of overhung grass...these are the nooks and crannies where trout rise. A simple glance might not reveal them. With so much river bank, the eyes must not just scan but stare extra long at such hiding places. A slower rising pace by the fish, obstructions they use for cover, and rippling bank reflections all inhibit your ability to see them. I know this oh so well since I am a fish hunter by nature. I fish twelve hours a day most every day during the guide season, from April through November. Non-stop staring is the name of the game between hatches, for there are most always risers to be found somewhere.

There are benefits to finding between-hatch fish besides the obvious thrill of the hunt. Trick casts might be needed to sneak trout out of cover and eddying currents. Successes are particularly gratifying and the trout are often on the big side of average. The same trout that was locked on to one insect type, being extra picky during the thick of the hatch now lessens its refinements. With less to choose from, a wider array of patterns might fool the trout, from size 22 Trico spinners to size 6 hoppers. Fish seem to "get dumb" between hatches, though exacting casts might be needed to extract them. It's the dry-fly angler with the best eyes that often wins the day.

In many places and currents, fish are easier to see when you are crouching low and looking upstream than when looking down or across. The way a large trout's head pushes up against the current seems to make it more well defined when viewed from below, especially in small waves or mixing currents. Direction, altitude, background lighting and reflections, and other viewing considerations can be manipulated by moving your position in relation to a hot-looking spot. You may need to cross and recross streams, both for better viewing and casting. Good eyesight and patience are key.

By applying your will, resolve, and the simple tools of the trade, limitless fishing horizons open up before you. Where once you just walked up and "fished," you now stalk, absorbing the trout's habits and habitats into an ever-growing arsenal of knowledge. Trout you may have routinely walked by before now play a large role in your daily outings. You anticipate hatches and feeding behavior. The full scope of their habitat and wanderings now play more into your hands.

Where to Look

Where do I look for trout? That is a compelling question. Trout are where you find them, as an old scribe once said, but some places are better than others.

The basic rule for finding river trout—whether rising, seen, or unseen—is to look to the sides of main and secondary currents. Trout, and especially large, plump, and desirable trout, don't want to sit there fighting the main force of the current. They lay off to the sides of it or fin underneath it, along the bottom of the river. Even in the heaviest flows, there is little current and many vertical eddies along a boulder-strewn streambed. In places like New Zealand, where the water is clear as air, even these trout are sight-fished. In our corner of the world, most fish will be out of our sight-fishing domain—but not all of them. Indicator nymphs and appallingly-heavy Buggers do the deed.

Having dispensed with these deep fish for the moment, we'll go back to those that concern us most; those finning and weaving, nosing and splashing to the sides of varying currents. Trout want relief from fast water, an abundant food supply brought to their front door, and either protective cover or an easy escape route. Larger rising specimens often reside in the slowest and sometimes shallowest water, where bugs pile thick and a caressing current winds around their snout. Life is good, and now many of these big bank-huggers are too large for birds to pick up.

Clear water means good sight-fishing. Deep-water trout can be out of the sight-fishing realm in some places. In other locales, such as clear, wilderness headwater rivers, even these fish can be stalked. Gaining an elevated viewing position helps. The fish will probably have to be "sight-nymphed". Pictured here is a New Zealand run. The water there is so clear trout can usually be seen in any depth.

During a good hatch, trout often drop into "tailouts" (shallow lower ends of pools), edgewaters, and inside bend "flats" to rise. These rising trout are along the slow, shallow, inside bend flat of a long pool. (Yes, others were under the willows.) Trout here don't have to fight much current and get plenty of fly to feed on. Flat-water fish often require finer tippets and exacting fly patterns to fool.

The edges (both sides) of a main current can be in a variety of places. In a straightway, it can be equal distance from both banks, leaving a wide, yet flowing slick a number of feet out from both shores. During a dense hatch, fish may eagerly push right out to the edge of faster water, capitalizing on current-borne food. Some risers, especially the larger ones, may remain in slower water and eddy lines peeling off the banks. Remember, trout like banks.

During a profuse hatch, trout can be seen from bank to heavy current edge and anywhere in-between. What I have observed in many places is that the largest risers stay out of the currents, but the smaller, eager, and more ignorant youth will go out and battle it,

reveling in the food and fast water. Many times you can choose the size of a fish caught by its position in the current and the size of its nose and wake.

Along river bends, currents tend to push to the outside of the bend (centrifugal force). Now the edges of the main current are in different locations. On the outside bend, where it piles into the bank, the edge of the main current is now a narrow strip tight to shore. Since the water is faster here, larger rocks, boulders, and logs usually get deposited or dropped from high-water currents in this zone. The classic case finds a narrow, swift, and food-filled lane swirling along excellent "pocket water." The larger rocks produce

Current edges always appeal to trout. On this sharp bend at the head of a pool, trout could be along the extended eddy line on the inside bend or on the one tight to the cliff where this trout was rising. Trout love to sit in slower water but face into a current that brings them food. PMD (pale morning dun) mayflies were the menu item here, a primary hatch across the West.

An incoming riffle drop-off, deep water, and overhead cover... this pool has it all. Everyone recognizes the most obvious spots where a trout might hold. Scrutinize the more subtle spots to catch fish you'd otherwise walk by or spook. Secondary currents and foam lanes, drop-off edges, changes in bottom strata, flats and eddies... such are the places you might find additional trout to heighten your day.

swirling back-eddies, little foam pools, and interesting nooks that hide some larger trout. This is typically a great area for upstream dry-fly fishing, both for sighted fish and for fishing blind. The dry-fly/nymph-dropper rig works well here too.

On the other side of the river, the edge of the main current may swing out to midstream. This usually forms a well-defined eddy line, typically holding fish. This can be a prime location to dry-fly fish during a hatch or spinner fall, with many trout eagerly giving their positions away.

A distinct eddy or flat is usually found at the head of the pool behind it the inside bend eddy lines, known to some as "the eye of the pool." Gravel and fine sand are deposited along this slower side of the stream. Fish can be dispersed over a wider area, and are sometimes visible hovering over the fine sediment bottom. During a hatch, large trout might not be so bank oriented here. Shorelines can be extremely shallow beaches. Good trout could be anywhere across this mellow flowing eddy, following foam lanes, or pushing out to the eddy line where the hatch might be thickest. Even when big eddy banks look coverless and feature-less, do not discount the possibility of big trout lying there. If a subtle secondary current runs back upstream and along it, and if there is a good supply of incoming fly (a hatch) and four-plus inches of water to hold in, trout can feed where few would

expect them to. Look for the noses, remembering that trout love secondary currents in big eddies.

What you're really looking for are ideal lodging places to the sides of main currents. An undercut bank with a foam lane and bushes for overhead cover would be an easily recognizable spot. A sprinkling of boulders or weed beds between the current edge and bank catches the eye too. Some prime locations are easily perceived, others are more subtle. It's the latter you want to study a little more, as you and everybody else has probably hammered away at the most obvious zones. Look at these areas anyway, and try finer tippet and small, novel patterns in heavily fished places.

When the river is busy I'll often consciously seek out the *second best* looking edges. I'm usually working out of a boat, where you can position yourself to fish either side and from any angle. Chances are, if several boats have gone before me, most if not all of them have cast to the exact same places—the most alluring edges of the main current or bank eddy lines. Though a number of rods have gone down the river, they've only covered a small and obvious percentage of the whole. The remainder of the river's trout still fin in comparative quiet and bliss. Choosing the second or even third best looking lies can produce good results.

Edges of the main current are certainly not the only game in town. Secondary currents can be preferred by trout for their easier flow, shallower habitat, and as great deliverers of food. On large rivers, the edges of secondary currents are among the best spots. Examples of secondary currents include the back-flowing ripple lines and food lanes in big eddies; smaller side channels around islands; and mini-channels through gravel bars or weed beds that filter into drop-off zones. Any mellow current carrying food into a good trout holding spot should be closely scrutinized, both for rises and subsurface fish.

In big water, trout like to cut their world down to size. The whole river seems like too big a universe for fish to call home.

Ripple lines that peel off points, inside bends, islands, rocks, or what have you, are favorites of trout. While ripple lines look like swift water to some, they're actually places where the main current loses velocity in shallower water. Here trout find plenty of food, overhead cover (in the form of choppy water), and calmer bottom undulations in which to hold. Most nymphs require high levels of oxygen, which is found in the swift, churning water of riffles. Hatching insects are profuse here as well. This riffle line of rising trout feasts on Trico spinners. Note that the fish's eyes actually come out of the water when they "headrise". Also note the bubbles of fish that just rose and went down, evidence of their feeding activity.

They'll seek out small side channels, mini-channels scooped out of a gravel and weed bed bottom, or ripple lines peeling off points. Trout can stay in the same area all summer, after returning from spawning or the effects of high water. Once you learn productive areas, chances are they'll continue to be good. Wherever insect-rich riffles flow into deeper pools is where a trout might call home.

Ripple and eddy lines peeling off points, bank protrusions, heads of islands, and the like are prime stalking grounds. Aquatic insect populations are high in swift, shallowish waters. The eddy on the inside of a ripple or eddy line makes a good home for trout, and sometimes schools of them. These are places to stare at for a good length of time. If a hatch is thick, riseforms can be obvious. Between hatches, trout might still rise, but less often and at an irregular pace. The heads and tails of trout can also be hard to see in the wavelets of the eddy line, even when they are steadily feeding. Crouching low and staring intently can cause fish to materialize where you had seen none before. Search from bank to ripple, from close to far. A trout seen rising between hatches is often a trout soon caught. They're looking for food. A well-placed, well-chosen fly can bring immediate results. It could take minutes to spot these fish, though, and to assess their feeding behavior.

Bank protrusions such as rocks, tree roots, logs, or a chunk of turf offer excellent trout-spotting locations. Rising and subsurface fish might be easily seen. Some "lay out" or rise in open sight. Others lay tight to cover, just briefly showing signs of their presence. Those holding really tight to cover go unseen by the majority of anglers that go by. Just the trout's snout may be visible, easing up from under a floating weed bed. Just the slightest hump of water might give it away. Many times I have found bank-huggers by first seeing a big bubble floating down the shoreline, with no apparent

This trout is holding upstream of a large, rectangular boulder. His tail is to the rock and his nose to the incoming foam line. Here he sees all the food and has an easy escape route, fast forward and into deeper water. Larger feeding trout are just as likely to be upstream of or alongside boulders, as they are to be downstream of them. If your visibility is poor, fish all three locations.

cause for its existence. Keen trout-stalkers know that such bubbles are commonly left by rising trout, caused by the air that escapes their gills after ingesting a surface morsel. They always take some air in too, expelling it as they settle back down into their watching-and-waiting position.

When guiding, I've noticed that most people think trout only hold downstream of rocks (bank edge or midriver rocks) or bank protrusions. When trout are looking for food though, they're pretty evenly split in their chosen current-watching positions, either upstream of, alongside, or downstream from a current-blocking obstacle. Many fish prefer the upstream location, with their tail in front of the rock. Here, they see all the food coming, are comfortable sitting in the "pillow" of calm water found just upstream of a structure, and have an easy escape route figured out (straight forward and out into deeper water). Trout commonly choose such upstream eddies, especially when overhead cover is added to the lot. This could be floating weed beds, a logjam, bushes, or just leaning grass. A good hatch makes these trout ideal targets.

Trout also like to tuck in tight alongside rocks, logs, and what have you. They have direct overhead and side cover, and an excellent feed lane trickling overhead. If floating down a river, I'd always try the upstream side of a rock first, then drift the fly tight to my side of it, and lastly drop another shot or two in the eddy behind it. When wading, you'd likely fish this in the reverse order. In this way, you've covered all the bases.

There are many "flats" on a river that trout favor. Currents are moderate. Breaks in it for fish cover come from weed beds, rocks, or undulations in a gravel streambed. Flats between one and four feet in depth have plenty of food, insects, room to live and move,

A trout feeds off an eddy line along a deep boulder-strewn bank, in this case one made by man to curb erosion along a highway. Outside bends, where larger rocks and logs are dropped by swift currents, are the natural areas for this. Rock slides off steep, river-cut hills also drop boulders along outside bends. Any deep eddy with a concentrated food lane going by is a good place to look. Trout often hover just under the surface, keeping an eye out for food.

This shallow-water trout's "smoke trail" is evident as he screams toward mid river. Feeding in just inches of water, he fell for a cautiously presented CDC caddis. Intermittent weed beds, rocks, and undulations in the streambed gravel give fish current breaks to feed from. This is the same water a beginning angler might brazenly wade through in an effort to cast to mid stream. These fish go to the observant, as many people wouldn't expect big trout in such shallow waters.

and are easy to rise in when hatches are on. Flats that appear dull and lifeless mid-day can be alive with scattered risers when conditions are favorable.

Such flats appear along inside bends, where the main current pushes to the far side. Tailouts, or the bottom ends of pools are prime rising flats in a hatch. The main current fizzles to a slow glide, shallowing and widening. These often appear just upstream of island systems (trout like it here), or before the drop-off into the next run and pool. Fish can rise all the way across the river in a tailout flats, even on the largest rivers where tailouts are at times a little less obvious in all that water. Other flats are found up and downstream of midriver gravel bars, in slower back channels, and across expansive eddies. Anywhere currents slow down and water depth lessens is a place trout might be found rising when the time is right. Walking or floating slowly and looking carefully is the name of the game. Flats can be quite large and there are often scattered fish to be found. Where flats slow and shallow to a near standstill, cruising trout might be found. If you can gain a little elevation, the light is right, and wind chop isn't inhibiting your subsurface viewing, good sport can be had casting to cruisers between hatches.

On rich rivers, weed beds commonly grow across fine-graveled trout flats. These support numerous aquatic insects and crustaceans, also providing good breaks from the current. Trout here come alive at hatch time but can be difficult to spot beneath the water mid-day. There are fish that continue to rise sporadically,

even when the hatch is mostly gone. Look all the harder at these times. The observant angler usually catches some bonus rising fish.

Lake edges and flats can support rich weed beds and cruising trout to be sight-fished. Scuds, cressbugs, damselfly and *Callibaetis* nymphs, leeches, snails, and midge pupae make up the bulk of their subsurface diet. Midges, *Callibaetis*, and Trico mayflies, damselflies,

Deep water and slow foam lanes should draw your eye. Trout, or as in this case schools of trout, can reside in such places. They might be seen rising or finning subsurface. Constantly remind yourself to scan the entire river for likely scenarios. Keep your eyes moving, though slowly and with purpose.

A "slough cruiser" slowly works his way through shallow water and shadows. Such trout are very aware of their surroundings, a bit twitchy, but great fun to sneak up on. Fine leaders and realistic patterns can be necessary, as these fish see so well in the still water. Unless they're feeding aggressively, failures are just as likely as victories here. By squatting, kneeling, and keeping low, and by using sloth-like movement, anglers can get within easy casting range. It's often best to cast way ahead of the fish, letting it come to your fly.

caddis, and hoppers make up most of the surface fare. Fishermen looking for big trout turn much of their attention to the many productive lakes and spring-fed ponds across the West.

Deep, slow river pools and runs frequently have foam/food lanes wandering across their surface. Individual or schools of trout hang beneath them at times, rising to spent insects or freshly hatched ones. Bugs accumulate in scum lines, remaining a big food source long after the hatch wanes. When the sun is high, these fish can be easily seen underwater too. Many floating anglers overlook midriver foam lanes because they're too focused on the banks. Wade fishers can't reach some of them. When fishing or when looking for fish, remind yourself to occasionally scan the entire river scene. It's easy to pass by actively-feeding fish if you don't keep looking in every quarter.

Big, shallow eddies and large sloughs connect to rivers in places, often where high-water side channels retreat from during normal flows. Some have springs entering, providing more constant and comfortable temperatures year round. Trout can cruise such sloughs like they would a lake. In the heat of summer they'll hang around the springs. Many anglers walk by shallow sloughs, not thinking trout would dwell in such places. They're always worth a look though, especially mid-day, when the viewing is good, and river hatches are likely on the wane. One, a few, or many trout could reside there, usually cruising into plain sight for the cautious observer. You want to sneak up and watch from a camouflaged position. Spend a few minutes at least studying the scene.

"Slough cruisers" tend to be adult fish with their own cruising territory. Some are protective of their "beats," chasing other fish off. Six inches to a few feet is all the water they need, especially if weed beds offer cover. Trout can slink in and out of view through weed growth, the shadows and limbs of bank cover, or even by cruising back and forth from river to slough. This is pure sight-fishing excitement, and is worth the effort of looking for it.

My first real addiction to slough cruisers blossomed in New Zealand, where such fish are common in numerous eddies. Almost every New Zealand slough has at least one wary resident fish and often more. Some swim looking at the surface for food. Some swim tilted down, nose to the bottom. Others glide on an even keel, looking everywhere for both food and danger. These clear-water trout are tough to fool at times—occasionally even impossible—but are always intriguing. Fish of 18 to 26 inches are the norm there, and you see every move they make. Dapping (letting the line, leader, and fly straight down) from weeping willows to slough cruisers became a personal sideline. Even the expression on their face when you set the hook from above is clear as can be. This was great fun (both for me and anyone watching).

Applying clear-water lessons learned in New Zealand to water in the U.S. proved that these were universal trout traits. Local sloughs, especially where ground water seeps in, produced similar results. Regional slough cruisers range from 10 to 23 inches, not bad for those that take the time to look. Expect picky and spooky fish though, and some interesting angling challenges.

Some other sweet spots to keep a close eye on include mini-channels formed in shallow water by the shifting of streambed gravel. Side-slipping currents in particular can carve mini-channels along banks or from there on out to the main current edge. Winter ice can shove riverbed gravel around, producing ridges, undulations, and mini channels of various types. Some are enhanced by

Keep low and wait. A slough cruiser could very well come into view. These fish have routine paths they follow called "beats". It could take many minutes for a fish to show up "on beat", and for you to learn its pattern before planning your cast. Stealth and patience are a must, as are controlled and delicate casts.

Bank & Eddy Fish Locations

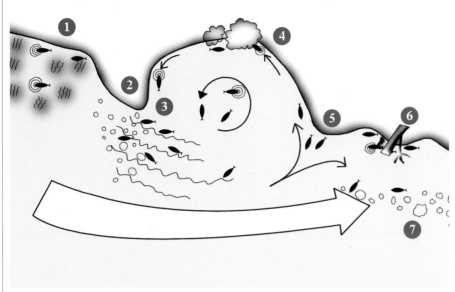

1. Tailout flats are good fish-stalking grounds, especially during a hatch. Fish can be along shallow, featureless edgewaters, or scattered anywhere across ths flats. Weed beds are often found here.
2. Ripples and eddy lines peeling off points are hot spots on any trout stream, and especially on big tailwater or dam-controlled rivers. Numbers of fish might be found here, rising or subsurface. This is one location that deserves good blind-fishing coverage if no fish are seen. Nymphs are usually most productive.
3. Eddies attract trout. Look for foam lanes and secondary current edges. Trout can hang in the calm middle eddy, along the banks, and along the river's main current edge.
4. Shade, overhung, and deep banks all offer trout cover. They can be more difficult to see in shade, even when rising, so pay extra attention.
5. Where the current spilts to form an eddy is a zone many anglers overlook. Much of the current-borne food passes by this juncture before rotating upstream.
6. Fish might be found upstream of, alongside, and downstream from bank obstructions. The floating weed mat on the upstream side of this log deserves an extra look. Fish can be partially hidden under the floating weeds.
7. Drop-offs near the edge of the main current generally hold fish. They might not be visible unless they're rising, or if you can gain a higher spotting elevation.

flowing water over the summer. These can be seen as a difference, or darkening of water color among the golden streambed gravel. Trout really like mini-channels and will reside in potholes too.

Where a current edge hits the bank and divides into an eddy, where part of the current eases downstream and part upstream into the eddy itself, there lies a quiet pocket of water that's perfect for trout. Fish in this splitting-currents location get all the food coming into their front door, before it goes up- or downstream. A bit of foam often lingers there. Any overhead cover is a bonus. This is a bug-rich hotspot that many anglers overlook.

Drop-offs, converging currents, mini-channels bisecting gravel bars, weed bed breaks, insignificant-looking bank eddies...the trout-stalking possibilities go on and on. Every reach of river is different. Each river's fish have their own idiosyncrasies. There are trout to be found. By stalking, hunting, and searching both the surface and beneath, many trout begin to reveal themselves to your now-focused eyes and mind. Habits and feeding preferences are learned, that information mentally cataloged for future use.

Trout will surprise you too, zooming out from shallow-water haunts you'd never expect them in. Never let your stalking guard down. Figure out why they're in such places. Pump the stomachs of netted fish. Look closely at the aquatic life. This learning process is almost as enjoyable as catching fish.

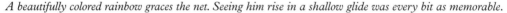

A beautifully colored rainbow graces the net. Seeing him rise in a shallow glide was every bit as memorable.

Chapter 3
Riseforms

A nice trout takes an autumn Baetis *mayfly. Riseforms can tell you a lot about the trout's size and give a clue as to what it's eating. Note the squirt of water, a result of the roof of its mouth coming down on the surface during the rise.*

Rings on the water...they catch the angler's eye and define the sport. The aftereffects of a rise, the fading wakes, don't tell you much though. Watch a little longer. Make a mental image of the riseform itself. This fleeting moment, when the trout first breaks the surface, can tell you several things. It's often possible to tell a trout's size, what it's eating, and the direction it's facing by the way it rises. It's not a foolproof system, fish behavior can vary a bit from river to river and species to species, nonetheless, riseforms can be signposts to success.

Sips are often seen with midging trout. Here, several are working the edge of a current line, where food is concentrated. Some sips are made by small trout. Other times, the easy rings can mask a large yet subtle feeder. The size and pulse of the resulting wakes can give away the fish's true size.

Sips

Sips are seen as quiet, often steady riseforms in still or gliding waters. The trout hover just beneath the surface, quietly inhale morsels, which are usually on the small side or can't get away. No nose or head is seen in the air, no fins or back, and no splash or humping of the water takes place. In some places and during certain times, sippers tend to be small fish, making such little head rises that they're too small to see. Other times, larger fish rise this way, with so little body movement that the lack of resulting wakes belies their true size. Midges and midge emergers, plus small spentwings and terrestrials, are likely targets of sipping trout.

If there are several sippers in close proximity, watch their riseforms and timing for a while. Look for the fish that makes the biggest, slowest wakes. Slow pulsing wakes mean larger fish. The biggest ones are often in the slowest and sometimes shallowest water, where they don't have to fight the current. At times smaller fish are more willing to feed further out into the current.

Check the river's surface for hatches to match. If a trout doesn't take your fly after a few good presentations, lengthen and lighten your tippet, use a smaller or different fly, or perhaps cast to them from a different angle. I like to cast down and across to flat water sippers, using a reach cast, which shows them the fly before the leader. Also, allow a little time between presentations if the fish is showing any signs of getting nervous. Rest him periodically. Don't let stillwater fish see your line in the air either, or the water that sprays off it when false casting. False cast away from your fish and lead it by as far as necessary to keep it from seeing your cast.

A downstream reach cast is being performed by an angler on a mid-river flat. He's casting downstream, but as the line goes through the rod's eyes, he's "reaching" the rod back upstream as far as he can. When the line lands, he drops the rod tip and follows the line on downstream with it. This shows picky fish the fly before the leader, which is critical in fooling some of them.

⤙ Stalking Western Trout ⤚

(A trout sipping steadily in a ripple line may take casts just inches away from their nose. Those in a flat may need to be led by six feet, or even more.)

Sippers are often small to average size fish, but now and then a brute will surprise you. The few times my fly has disappeared with almost no rings in evidence, it's been larger than average brown trout that did the deed. A few seem to have the ability to inhale bugs off the surface with minimal disturbance.

Splashers

Splashing, slashing riseforms can be due to several condition factors. For instance, in the spring, when trout are just starting to rise for the year, some seem suspicious of the surface. They can rush up to grab flies, scurrying quickly for the safety of the depths or cover after each rise. A splashy riseform might be seen, regardless of the hatch. The same fish come midsummer would be making confident head rises to the hatch du jour.

Other splashes are seen when quick emerging insects like certain caddis or fast-water mayflies are found. The trout rush up to grab the emergers just as they reach the surface. Many aquatic insects spend almost no time resting on the surface before flying off. These are the ones that solicit splashy rises. Splashing and boiling trout can indicate the need to use emerger patterns, either dead drifted, swung down and across the currents, or hung beneath a dry fly.

Large insects can also bring forth splashy rises, especially when there are but few around, or if the event has just started up for the year. Salmonflies, green drakes, traveler sedges in lakes, damselfly adults, hoppers, and October caddis are cases in point. Even extra-large trout, who are usually discreet and energy-efficient feeders, can make a rush for these oversized insects. The size of the splash and resulting wakes give the trout's size away. Larger twitched or even skid fly patterns could be the ticket here.

This angler is readying his gear as a trout "porpoises". Such fish are often feeding subsurface on the slow-emerging nymphs or pupae of midges and mayflies. Some "resting" caddis pupae can also be targeted by fish, pupae pausing beneath the surface before their final molt and launch to a brave new world. The trout's nose doesn't poke above the surface but their back, dorsal fin and tail can. Other porpoising trout could be taking surface and subsurface food. In this case, their nose or head should be visible above the surface, at least part of the time, and a bubble left behind.

Small and fast-water trout tend to be splashers too, with larger trout often holding in slower water off to the sides, tight to some structure, or hanging down in the tailout of a pool. Be sure to scan the whole scenario before rushing in. The bigger rising fish can usually be identified with patient observation.

Porpoising Trout

Porpoising refers to trout whose back and tail glide up and out of the water. Sometimes their head is seen, sometimes not. This is an easy, graceful motion, indicating that the fish are intercepting slower rising emergers just under the surface. Midges are often on the

Splashy riseforms can be due to a nervous, grabby fish rushing to the surface, or when trout take some larger food items with gusto. Certain quick-emerging aquatic insects also bring splashy rises, as the fish have a very limited emergence "moment" in which to procure the insect. In the latter case, emerger patterns are most likely to succeed, perhaps fished as a dropper off a dry fly.

Note the bubble left behind, riding the wake of this trout's riseform. This generally confirms that he fed off the surface, and not from just underneath it. I've often located inconspicuous rising fish by finding such bubbles first. This is especially true along bushy banks and in chop lines, where rises can be masked by their surroundings. This bubble of air was vented out of the fish's gills, air it took in when ingesting a fly.

Trout taking nymphs or pupae a little further below the surface can still disturb it. These bulges, humps, and swirls definitely point to the nymph or emerger fishing option. One fished below a dry fly (as a strike indicator) is a good way to go. Some fish will take either. Both porpoising and bulging trout can be very picky and focused on one particular food type. Check on the current hatches beforehand, and have at least a couple emerger options available.

menu. *Baetis*, PMD, and other slow-swimming mayfly emergers are key players. Fly patterns of choice tend to be in the 16-24 size range. Such trout can be very picky. Have some emerger patterns on hand. Fishing one as a dropper off a small but visible match-the-hatch dry fly is a good way to go. Think 6X.

Sometimes porpoising trout will be taking both surface and subsurface food. A bubble is usually left behind on the surface after an actual rise. The trout takes in some air along with the fly on the surface. This air is vented out the gills as it goes back down. Porpoising/rising trout do have a way of dispersing this telltale bubble though, as their back and tail glide through it.

Most porpoising trout are feeding steadily, often with a well-defined rhythm, as can be true of rising trout. It can be a very lazy rhythm too. Note it and time your fly's dance to that of the fish. Since most porpoising trout are of at least moderate size, running to lazy and large, be prepared to fight them accordingly on your light tippet. Pause half a second before setting the hook, allowing the fish to tilt down. Set it by just tightening up firmly, not with a "bass slamming" jerk. Then be instantly ready to clear the line around you and let the fish run. Don't clamp the line to the rod handle or put a death grip on the reel. Five to 7X won't take a lot of abuse when chafing on an oversized, head shaking, and toothy trout. Let it have its first couple of runs. Pressure it steadily thereafter, always ready to release the reel handle on a surge. Porpoising trout can be memorable trout, presuming you can fool them!

Bulgers

Trout intercepting emerging nymphs a little deeper under the surface can cause it to "bulge". The trout doesn't break the surface with any part of its body, but it does move enough water to disturb it, giving itself away to any nearby anglers. A swirl, boil, or bulge results, indicating the activity below. You might also see flashes under the water as a twisting, turning trout catches both nymph and piercing sunbeams. If the light is right, and high enough in the sky, you might be able to see said trout under water most of the time.

Bulging trout are most often seen with medium to fast emerging insects, and ones that don't spend much if any time riding on

the surface. Caddis and pale morning dun mayflies (in certain conditions) come quickly to mind. Some trout bulge to PMD emergers, where in other places they might porpoise, or rise to the duns. Sometimes they bulge, porpoise, and slash across weedy riffle areas where the flies are actually emerging, with sippers and head risers found on downstream in slow, deep pools, where nothing but duns and cripples are available (few PMDs are actually hatching there). Different parts of the river can show different hatches, stages of hatches, and trout behavior, all during the same timeframe.

Wakes

Once in a while you see serious wakes, not of a fish you spooked (which is more common), but of those chasing larger, active food items. Crayfish, sculpin, damselfly nymphs, minnows and the like are common prey. Though somewhat rare, there have been those times when a streamer or crayfish pattern tossed immediately in a waker's path has brought instantly delightful results. Of course you must have such a fly ready and pre-rigged on a backup rod. For me, this has usually been a boat affair, with extra rods loaded and ready to go. This isn't something you see every day. Being on the water a lot and looking ups your odds.

Head Risers

Now we're talking. This is the good stuff. Once trout reach a certain size, say 13- to 14-plus inches, they begin rising in a more dignified manner. Should the hatch or spinner fall be thick, they sidle off to the edge of the current, often tight to a bank, eddy line, or willow, and set up a rhythmic feeding pace. They hover just under the surface, tipping their head up to engulf the fly. It's not a sip you see. The top of the trout's head comes completely out of the water. Even his eyes become completely exposed to air. The roof of his mouth comes up and over the insect. It then slaps down on the surface making a little popping sound. All is good with the world.

In some fishing circles, the search for rising fish means "hunting heads." The bigger fish do slow head rises and make big, slow wakes. Smaller trout sip and splash, making little wakes. Look for the heads!

"Head risers," the term becomes obvious with this photo. The trout's upper jaw (and thus entire head) comes up and over the fly, capturing it. Their eyes even come completely out of the water. Close observation easily reveals them on stream. Head rising is confined, or at least only visible with fish of about 12 inches and up. Sixteen- to 22-inch trout are the most obvious "head risers," and the most alluring targets! Note the Trico spinners about to go down the trout's gullet.

Some trout, especially browns, will follow a fly downstream a bit, inspecting it before they decide whether it's good enough to eat. The rise that follows can be almost straight up, with both jaws lunging into the air. When perfomed by trout 20 inches or more, it makes for a most enthralling act. We've had browns to 28 inches take flies this way. It's guaranteed to stir an angler's heart!

As a general rule, the bigger the fish, the bigger and slower the head rise. When the bugs are at their thickest, the pace will pick up a bit, but the pace of a big fish is still likely to be slower than that of a smaller one. Topping the insect list for what brings up head risers are (in seasonal order): midges, *Baetis* mayflies, grannom caddis, western March browns, pale morning dun mayflies, spent caddis (spotted sedge, long horn sedge, etc.), Trico mayfly duns and spinners, bonus terrestrials mixed in with the last three, and autumn *Baetis*. Other hatches could certainly bring up all the head risers, these are just the most universal ones across the west.

Naturally, you need a stream, river, or lake with plentiful to obscene hatches and large trout to get the full head-riser effect. In New Zealand backcountry rivers, where trout average about 23 inches commonly running up to 28 inches, head rising is taken to perhaps its ultimate level. Large trout there rise oh so slowly. Big heads, with both jaws languishing in the crisp, dry air unnerve the inexperienced. The old saying is to recite "God save the Queen" before setting the hook. This is how long it takes such big headed browns to sink back down after their slow motion rise to a dry fly.

Back home in the west, the trout may not average so large but there are a lot more of them. Fourteen- to 24-inch risers are widely scattered. Head-hunting here is a worthy sport and usually addicting. I know several anglers who will never cast unless a big head is sighted.

The funny thing about head risers is that their eyes usually come completely out of the water on each rise. I have many photos illustrating this point. Do the trout see you then? It's hard to blink without eyelids. Perhaps they enjoy seeing both worlds—the heavy, flowing, and homey water world, and the brilliant, acrid, and dangerous upper one. Or perhaps I've spent too much time on the water...

Straight-Up Head Rise

This is a sideline affair, seen now and again, but so enchanting that such trout linger in the memory a good, long while. Larger trout will sometimes drop back a bit inspecting a potential meal, before rising almost straight up to procure it. The whole head, both jaws agape, heave towards the sun. Many seem to sink back down slowly tail first, before refacing the current. You must wait till they sink and straighten before setting the hook (God save the Queen). There seems to be a tendency for these fish to be big-toothed, head-shaking browns (browns to 27 inches have been taken on dries locally). They have a way of rasping leaders with their teeth and winning some protracted battles, even on 3X. Always check your tippet for worn spots after each trout landed. Retie the fly if there's any doubt.

Gulpers

Take your common "head riser," add a couple hundred thousand flies, maybe a few rising buddies willing to share the glut, and you have the classic "gulper" scenario. Trout become somewhat excited

Trout that head rise rapidly to Trico spinners are known as "gulpers." These can be found in both rivers and lakes. Mid-morning to early afternoon, from mid-July to early September is the time frame. 6-7X tippets and size 20-24 fly patterns are the ticket. As the spinner fall wanes and the fish are still looking, the same trout might go for size 16 Parachute Adams and such. Every fishery will have its own demands. In remote waters, 5X and size 18s could get all the results you want during the heat of the hatch.

Nature's glut, a vast sheet of Trico spinners coat the water. This mid-morning event brings most trout rivers alive come summer. Many fish (or all of them) can be rising. Look for the biggest ones, off to the sides of the main current and up against slow-water banks.

by the unlimited but time-constrained food supply. Maximizing their opportunities is the name of the game (a little like humanoids). Trico spinners are the typical gulping menu item. Millions of tiny size 20-24 spentwings literally coat the surface. The view from beneath must be that of prismatic wing imprints like stained glass, peppered with tiny black bodies and tails. Trout begin to feed eagerly, pushing the head rising thing to its limit.

While each fish has its own particular way of doing things, patterns evolve. Trout tend to head-rise several times as fast as they can, then stop for a moment to work the flies down their gullet. When the light is right, you can see them opening and closing their mouths underwater, a yawning-like affair, to loosen the flies from their teeth, tongue, and gills. After this, they quickly get back to gulping. The whole time they're hovering just under the surface. One fish might rise eight times in as many seconds, then take a five-second break. Another might go with more of a one-rise-at-a-time cadence. Each fish is slightly different.

Gulping fish often are schooled-up at prime dining areas. The food is so plentiful that territorial aspirations are laid aside, at least for the moment (though some fish will chase each other around). All the fish in a big eddy might push up into the eddy line and feed together,

even rolling over each other. The term "pirhana pod" is one we're inclined to use, and it's not much of an exaggeration.

Gulpers are also found on lakes. Having no current, they make up for it by cruising (which they also do in big river eddies). Trico and *Callibaetis* mayflies are their fare. Midges add to the fray. Lake cruisers are a little more problematic to cast to, as they can randomly change direction or get herded around by fly lines.

The gulper period on most rivers and lakes runs from about early to mid-July to mid-September. Find the Trico spinner swarms paralleling the banks come mid-morning, and the head risers and gulpers should soon follow.

Tailers

This is another sideline affair, but in the right times (between hatches) and places (weed beds), trout can tail like redfish. They'll push their snout through the weed beds to dislodge scuds, cressbugs, and nymphs. Should the water be of a depth that's somewhat less than the trout's length, their tails can stick up in the air. They'll eat as they scour, or swim back through the area to vacuum the evacuees. Don't hold your breath while waiting for this action though. Hanging around the right habitat, shallow weedbeds, ups your chances.

When whitefish and trout are rising together, try to tell the heads from the tails. Larger trout will hover just under the surface, pushing their nose up above it in an easy glide. A slow-waking push is the usual result. Whitefish and small trout tend to splash—the juvenile trout with reckless abandon—and the whitefish as they dive for the bottom. Their tails often make a little splash as they wiggle back down. Whitefish also roll or quickly porpoise and splash. It's a little harder for them to take surface flies since their mouth is further under their head. Whites also school up, mostly in the centers of pools and tailouts. If you see a school of tail-flips, look for quieter rings and noises around its perimeter.

Telling Trout From Whitefish

Trout and whities generally rise differently. While there are times that you can't tell them apart, much of the time you can. Steadily rising trout tend to hover just under the surface and tip their nose up. A quiet sip or water-pushing head rise is what you see. Whitefish usually hold near the bottom, coming all the way up to

grab a fly, then wiggle their way back to the bottom again. What you see here is a little splash their tail makes while they accelerate back down. Sometimes you see their body roll up and over the fly (since their mouth is more on the underside of their head), followed by the little splash of the tail.

Whitefish school-up, mostly in the middle of pools or tailouts. Numerous tail flips and splashes indicate such a school. Juvenile trout can splash as well, and are often mixed in. Larger trout tend to be peripheral fish, working more quietly at the head, to the sides, and downstream of pool belly whitefish. They can be mixed together though. Then you must pick the slow-sipping noses from the swifter-flicking tails. The whitefish that fool me the most are individuals and small schools that move into slow, shallow eddies. Here they tend to porpoise like trout, rather than do the tail flip. Since they're not going down very deeply, they lose that splashy trademark. They can even sip just like a trout at times. We try to cast around whitefish, but get fooled now and then. Whitefish rise most from late fall, through winter, and into spring, when mature nymphs aren't so available. They make up for this loss by concentrating on midges in every stage, as well as grabbing all the small crustaceans they can. Cressbugs, snails, and the odd scud stay active in the coldest water, and help keep both the whitefish and trout's bellies full.

Telling a trout's size and food preference by its riseform takes a little practice and close observation. The rewards are worthwhile. The telling of size in particular is of great interest to anglers. Anything you can learn from their behavior and environs plays into your favor.

Sight-fishing success comes during a late-morning PMD/caddis/Trico session. Multiple hatches are common in summer. Some fish eat them all, others specialize. Different areas of the river can favor different feeding habits. A stomach pump, used routinely, can help you decipher the fishes preferences.

Chapter 4
Spotting Subsurface Trout

Late summer brings many sight-fishing challenges. In this slough-like back channel, several trout were cruising. (In higher water conditions they would have been holding in a stronger current.) The angler is staying back from the bank to avoid detection. One fish finally succumbed to a cased caddis imitation twitched along the bottom.

While spotting rising fish can be easy enough at times, finding subsurface ones will always take a little more time and concentration. Constant scanning and probing with the eyes is a workmanlike job. Keep them moving slowly and systematically.

Since this is primarily a between hatches, midday strategy, the sun becomes your ally. A sparkling illumination of the streambed is

Gaining a little elevation helps immensely when spotting subsurface trout. Here, a really nice trout cruises and pauses in a big bank eddy. Wearing drab clothing and making ultra-slow movements allow you to get close. Once you get down to the water to cast though, such fish can be lost to view. Mark them against some bank object to help pin down their location. Having a second angler act as a "spotter," staying above where the viewing is good, ups your odds when fish are cruising.

to your advantage, though the fish might be more comfortable with a hazy sky. Having the sun at your back is a big plus for viewing. From that vantage point the fish are well lit, and they have a harder time seeing you because the sun is in their eyes. If the sun is in your face, the shadow of the trout on the streambed might be the first thing you see. You'll be highly illuminated though, and easier for the fish to see. Be all the more stealthy when you're basking in the sunlight.

Polarized sunglasses and a brimmed hat are a must of course, as are a large degree of patience and determination. Proceed at a lazy pace. Don't break a sweat. Stop and stare carefully across likely areas, for trout can come slowly into focus. I've stared at the bottom of shallow runs for five minutes before big fish "materialized" before me. It's not a hasty game, especially if streambed rocks are fish sized. Most often, this isn't the case.

Besides having the sun at your back, it's of great benefit to have trees or a high bank on the far side of the river to block sky reflections and glare. On a small stream, this is commonplace. On large rivers and lakes it's only an occasional blessing, unless you're in a boat looking at the shore. At times you can move around to gain the best viewing perspective and backdrop.

Any altitude you can gain helps dramatically in locating fish. Sneak up on hillsides, but use available cover to mask your silhouette. Stand up in a boat if far enough away. But remember, if you can see them, they might be able to see you. On shore you can largely overcome the trout's ability to see you by wearing drab, camouflaging clothes (avoid bright clothes and reflective, shiny fishing trinkets). Move very slowly. Trout are most likely to spot motion first. Use available cover, either in front of, or behind you, masking your silhouette as much as possible. Crouch where needed, standing up slowly to look further away. Do everything in slow motion.

From a boat, the task is more difficult since it's harder to hide. Choppy water will disguise your presence to some degree. On calm flats, the fish have the advantage. Staying a long cast away is your best bet, while being as stealthy as possible. A low-profile, neutral-colored craft is better than a high-sided bright one. Float tubes and prams can get closer to spooky fish than a high-sided drift boat with a standing angler can. If the visibility is good, with the sun at your back and a high bank or trees before you to block sky glare, you may be able to stay seated and spot fish. Casting as far as you can with finesse ups your odds too. The skilled distance caster will catch more fish. Sloppy long casts of a dry fly or nymph will scare more fish than they'll fool though. There are many times when I see trout spook as the angler stands up to cast, especially if the boat is close to them. Learning the trout's "fear zone" of the boat is part of the overall strategy. This changes with water and light conditions, and when standing versus sitting.

The little wakes your boat pushes out in front of it can put very touchy fish down, as can the wakes from a wade-fisher's legs. All wakes and rowing sounds should be minimized to allow for the

If rising trout are sparse, streamer fishing allows you to fish and look for risers at the same time. Indicator nymphing might be a better bet, but then you have to glue your eyes to the bobber, unless you happen to have a rower to watch it for you. This 24-inch rainbow was a big bonus. Such fish are not an everyday occurence.

most secretive approach. Let the anchor down slowly. The sound of it thudding and dragging can scare fish too. Trout are wild animals, ever alert to any intrusion on their domain.

If you can't resist casting, but still want to look for fish, a Woolly Bugger, streamer, crayfish, leech, or damselfly nymph would be a good choice. You don't have to stare at these once you've presented them, as you would a dry fly or indicator nymph. When in a boat, you can even fish dries or indicator nymphs and have the rower watch your fly while you hunt visible fish. He can tell you when you have a hit and all bases will be covered. When feeling out the day's fishing from a boat, I'd have one angler use a nymph, perhaps as a dropper off a dry fly, and have the other angler use a streamer. You can test the trout's preferences and look for fish at the same time. Trout can be relatively easy to see from a boat as many are holding along banks and in eddies. The bank reflection blocks sky glare, and if the surface is choppy, you can stay reasonably close to them without being seen. Good vision, polaroids, and unwavering determination will reveal fish that most others float or wade by.

While you can certainly blind-fish all afternoon and in non-hatch periods, sight-fishing adds a new level of anticipation. You'll learn more about trout behavior and catch additional fish. You're more likely to spot bigger fish too, those being the easiest to see. The remembrance of sight-fishing victories seems to last much longer than those of any number of indicator-nymph-caught fish.

What to Look For

When hunting subsurface trout, you may or may not see a whole fish clearly. There are many subtle signs to be aware of. Movement is often the first sign. Trout can swing to the side to partake of a nymph in moving water. They might cruise eddies, sloughs, ultra-slow flats, and lake edges. They can rise in the water column, coming in and out of view, or pass from shadow to shadow along an overhung bushy bank. Any unusual or even suspected movement should instantly draw the eye's lingering attention.

Good Fish-Spotting Conditions

Sunlight penetrates water, illuminating fish and bottom.

Darkness or tall trees and hillsides block sky reflection making it easier to see fish under water. A hat and polarized sunglasses help immensely too.

A stalker's bird's-eye view reveals a nice brown holding along an edge-water. Can you see it? It's actually its shadow that defines this trout, which is often the case. Any fish-sized shape, shadow, difference in coloration, and of course movement should be more closely examined.

A difference in color is often the key. The green top and red sides of a rainbow sometimes shows through, contrasting with the brown-hued bottom. Even the camouflaging yellow/brown of a brown trout can be different enough to stand out at times. In other instances, the brown's coloration makes it almost invisible.

In this case, the shadow a trout casts on the streambed becomes your greatest benefactor. Mid day, such shadows can be bold and well defined. Any movement of the fish amplifies the effect. If the sun is in your face rather than behind you, the full shadow will fall on your side of the trout. It's common to spot trout shadows and scarcely be able to see the fish at all.

On cloudy days and at dusk and dawn your visibility into the water will be lessened. The trout's shadows will be minimized. Color differences fade too. Add some wind and the sight-fishing game can come to a near standstill. No worries, Bugger on. Look in wind-free slicks along banks, in eddies, and in the shadows of over-

A big brown cruises a slough. This one usually kept a "nose down" posture, hunting nymphs. Others "look up," expecting the surface to provide their food. Clear water makes them spooky customers. In high water and murky conditions, probe the slough with black Woolly Buggers and such.

hanging trees. Go slower, get higher, look harder, then experiment with blind-fishing techniques.

In many cases, you don't see a whole fish. Just the head or tail may be in view. Sometimes just the mid torso or fins are apparent but nothing else. Be alert to any part of a fish shape, especially where immediate cover is at hand. Trout will hover half under cut-banks, floating weed mats, and willow boughs. Parts of them can be camouflaged with streambed rocks while one end stands out. Only his waving tail may catch your eye. Any part of a trout's silhouette, color, or shadow could be your only clue.

Feeding fish often give their underwater positions away. The flash of a trout's side as it twists to grab a nymph can clearly point it out to you. Even if you can't focus on it under water, you now know where it is. An indicator nymph is likely to succeed if fished deeply enough. An occasional rise from a trout draws the eye's attention. It's often possible to see it beneath the water after that, especially in a moderate current where they tend to hold a feeding position. If you can't see it, at least you know it's there. A dry fly may bring him up. A dry-fly/nymph-dropper rig would be good here, matching the current hatches.

A rise in a slough or lake is another story. These trout cruise throughout the day since there's no current to bring them food. Stillwater trout usually have a territory or cruising pattern though. If you see several risers, you know you have something to work with. It may take time to figure out their "beat" and intercept them with a carefully presented fly. If the light, surface, and background viewing conditions are right, you may be able to see these fish much of the time as they fin their circuitous routes. Study them a while before casting.

If the choice is available, move to the most advantageous spotting position. Cross the stream or switch sides of the lake. Get the sun behind you. Gain a more elevated spotting position, but stay camouflaged and still. Any underwater motion or surface disturbance should draw your studious attention.

Where to Find Subsurface Trout

Spotting underwater fish is generally more limited than stalking risers. Naturally, it's the water closer at hand that usually allows better viewing. The slower the current and more even the surface, the easier trout come into view (and the more easily they see you). Slow water along inside bends of rivers, eddies, sloughs, and lake edges are prime spotting grounds. Choppier water has possibilities too, if well lit by the sun. Shallow riffles, drop offs (both parallel with the bank or across the current) , converging currents, foam lanes, and edgewaters are likely zones. Even deep, swift runs can reveal fish if you can gain an elevated and well-lit spot to look for them. Here are some of the prime lies.

Edgewaters

The banks of rivers are like magnets to trout. Deep, shallow, over-hung, coverless, swift, still...trout haunt them all. Those with good and obvious cover, with good current breaks, moderate depth, and a plentiful food lane dotted with foam are your best bets. Creep ever so slowly into viewing range, using available cover. Bank fish are extra wary. There are many bank- and tree-based predators that would love to eat them. Tiptoe, keep your rod pointed to the rear

Even banks with no apparent cover or character routinely hold fish. This is especially true on mellower flowing tailwater or dam-controlled rivers with high fish populations. What the fish find here is a certain velocity of water that's easy to hold in. Plenty of food comes by, and it's an easy escape route out to the depths. It's the size of these rivers that confuses some anglers. Huge runs mellow into giant tailouts. It's another example of trout being off to the sides of the main current but on a large scale, almost imperceptible to small-stream fishermen. Whether a bank run is swift with obvious boulder or turf pockets, or slow, wide and shallow, fish are likely to be found. Always search your bank from a slight distance, using available cover before walking right up to it and proceeding on.

Bank Protrusions

Add a rock, log, or turf clump to a bank, and it's almost certain a trout will take up residence there. Foam lines, eddies, and deep adjoining runs, up the anticipation level a notch higher. Stare at such places a good while. Since even post-hatch bugs and terrestrials linger on the water here, look for the occasional rise to give a trout's location away. Mark its position against a bank feature so you don't forget exactly where it is. Otherwise, stare beneath the surface bubbles and cover for the shapes and half shapes of fish.

Trout are just as likely to be upstream or alongside bank protrusions as they are to be downstream of them. There could be several trout in one or all of these locations. Study them all in turn, with an eye for the biggest fish. I usually give the upstream position the best odds. Fish there see all the food coming, have their backs to the wall, and can quickly bolt to mid-stream for safety. They get

Edgewaters of all types are utilized by trout. Stalking anglers can get good views of bank fish in many cases, as they're closest at hand. Move slowly, and don't let your feet outpace what your eyes can cover. A slowing current, foam lane, and protected holding location spells fish!

and out of sight, and have a lengthy look. Good spots are usually inhabited. Remember that trout are just as likely to sit upstream of a bank protrusion as they are downstream of it. If a good bank spot is part of a larger eddy, stare a little longer. Trout often cruise eddies, returning at regular intervals to favorite spots to hold for a few moments. Odds go to the patient angler.

An outside bend with eroded turf clumps provides excellent pocket water for trout. The edge of the main current is close to this bank, leaving a narrow strip of quieter water from which trout can feed. Food is concentrated here as well. On the other side of the river from this angler is the inside bend, a long, leading edge eddy line and a slow-water pool. This slow-water area is known to some as "the eye of the pool." It too is a prime trout spot of the first order.

"first dibs" on the food coming through that location and are often the largest specimens.

It's fairly common to have foam piled up on the upstream side of a bank protrusion. Food stacks up there too. Trout can hide beneath this foam or weed mat. Only their head might show. Sometimes it's only their nose occasionally heaving above the surface that gives their position away, and a big bubble left behind. Otherwise such fish can be completely out of view. This is a class 1 opportunity.

The problem is the casting position. If walking and working upstream, you may or may not be able to cast from behind the fish. Circle around, treading quietly and staying well back out of view. You can get a good fly first presentation from above, but then you have to stop the rest of the leader and line from going over it. Once the fly goes by, mend quickly toward midstream before retrieving. You may want to pause between presentations to keep the fish innocent. I prefer casting from midstream in this instance, whether wading or from a boat (don't let your wakes put it down). Being slightly upstream and using an exaggerated reach cast can win the day here.

Outside Bends

Bank protrusions and pocket water are common features of outside bends. Heavier currents force trout into a narrower slot of water. This makes stalking and blind-casting easier, since there's less to look over. Upstream of, alongside, and downstream of rocks, logs, and turf clumps offer classic trout opportunities. Concentrated bubble lanes deserve a second look. Boulders a little way off the bank but still inside the heaviest current are good big-fish locations too. Fish can be in any of the three choice positions here. Some like to feed from the current that flows between the boulder and bank, this being one of those premium secondary currents that trout love.

Outside bends of rivers are usually steeper than the beaches found on inside bends, giving higher fish-spotting positions. Do not let your feet proceed any faster than your eyes can thoroughly scan the waters. Fish will be somewhere along here and you can often

Movement was the key to spotting this trout. It's nymphing in an eddy off an outside bend. Note its "nose down" posture. Larger rocks deposited by high water currents and winter ice produce many a pocket that trout can call home along outside bends. Food is pushed by the water and concentrated here, giving fish plenty to choose from.

Trout Laying Upstream of a Rock

Feeding trout often hold upstream of boulders. There is a calm pocket there, where they can linger and watch food float by.

Fish hold upstream, beside, and under rocks, and in the eddy lines that peel off them. Fish these spots first, before tossing your fly in the eddy behind the rock as is usually done.

sneak quite closely up behind them (though those in eddies can be facing down river and right toward you). Look for submerged trout shapes, side-to-side movement, and the odd nose protruding from eddies. If no fish are seen, this is prime indicator nymph or two-fly water. Blind-fishing is likely to produce results.

Inside Bends

Inside bends tend to feature wide, slow water where fish are more scattered. They may be pushed up to the elongated eddy line, holding in the eddy, or be near the bank where food eases back upstream. This can take a bit of time to thoroughly examine. Many inside bend shorelines are beaches, especially at low water, making the viewing less than ideal at times, since you may not be able to gain much elevation. Offsetting this is the calm water and finer-grained bottom found here. Trout and their shadows can show up clearly, making good targets of themselves. Think out the casting approach and proceed with caution when fish are sighted. Flat-water fish are always easy to spook. Slack lining a deep nymph under an indicator is often the best approach, if they haven't shown a preference for dries.

The big eddy line at the head of an inside bend, where it swings off a point, is one of the true trout hot spots of the river. If subsurface fish can't be seen here, it's one place that deserves a thorough and systematic going through with an indicator nymph. Start in very close to the bank, working your presentations out a foot further each time. As you get deeper, add a second weighted nymph or more weight to the leader. Be ready for a take!

Inside bends downstream of the initial big eddy might feature extensive weed beds. The water here is moderate in depth and current. Look in and around them for weaving, flashing fish, and the occasional rise. When inside bend waters are slow enough, their trout might cruise. This can be a lot of water to look over. Stay alert for motion, color, and shadows in the water. Only the patient give inside bends their stalking due unless the trout are rising, yet

This angler is on the inside bend of this pool. Its expansive slower-water area can contain numerous scattered fish. On its near side, where the gravel is finer, trout or their shadows can show up easily. They might push up to the eddy line where the riffle drops in during a good hatch (both for the emerging nymphs and winged insects), or in the heat of summer for the added oxygen riffles produce. Trout can also drop over to the flats on the angler's side or tailout during a profuse hatch, where the rising is easier. Other good trout-holding spots here include the rock drop-off towards the opposite bank, where many pockets are formed. If no trout are spotted, the drop-in at the head of this pool and edges of its main currents certainly deserve to be probed with an indicator nymph.

at times subsurface fish are easy to see here if you stand and stare for a while. They can be in water as shallow as six inches.

One zone I've often seen big brown trout hold in is where there are changes in the streambed strata. Where silt or gravel changes to cobble is a good example. Browns will lay along this bottom change, presumably because it aids in camouflaging them.

This brown is holding and nymphing along a strata change, where gravel turns to larger cobble. Differences in current speed cause this (especially at high water), and browns in particular like to use such zones to camouflage themselves.

Current edges cause these, the slower area allowing finer grain sediments to fall out of the current. This attracts trout too. Such strata changes can also be the edge of a drop-off running parallel with the shore. These are commonly found along inside bends and deserve a good look. Expect trout to be nymphing here. Look for that side-to-side movement.

And speaking of the brown trout's love for camouflage, they'll often choose holding locations with a ripple line over their head. This hides them from winged predators. Even larger 20- to 23-inch browns will sit in very shallow water under the midday sun if a riffle line is overhead. They can be difficult to see here. Thus are some big, unseen browns caught blind along inside bends where ripple lines extend from banks or gravel bars.

I believe rainbows are far less camouflage conscious, and more dependent on speed and escape. I see far more rainbows cruising and holding in calm pools and eddies, finning near the surface for all the world and its predators to see. This is the opposite of the common conception "rainbows in fast water, browns in slow." What I see is brown trout using available camouflage options and rainbows caring less, or not at all. Thus the slow water can have easy-to-see 'bows, while riffle lines, rocks, streambed changes and such mask the wilier browns. They're all found in all the different water types, but their personalities and defense mechanisms vary.

Eddies and Sloughs

While I have mentioned eddies several times already, they deserve another look, for subsurface fish are likely to be seen here. Really large and spring-fed ones in particular deserve extra notice. Some

A trout cruises over a sunlit slough bed looking for food. Such trout will have "beats" they habitually travel, their own personal territories. A New Zealand trick for such fish involves waiting for them to swim away on their beat, casting a nymph and letting it sink to the bottom, then waiting for the trout to return. As they wander back along their familiar course, the nymph is twitched up out of the mud and catches their eye. Many will quickly accelerate to inhale the fly. Some are too wise, look at it, then flee from the scene. Slough fish are always a thinking angler's challenge.

eddies wander far back into part-time, high-water channel mouths. The fish behave like pond fish. While they can leave at will, they obviously have a liking for the eddy or slough environment. There's little or no current to fight, an ample food supply, constant year-round water temperatures where springs come in, and a place to call home. Slough-cruisers are great fun to stalk, but defeat is part of this game.

Since I pump a lot of trout's stomachs over the course of the season, the differences in food options and feeding habits becomes clearer. Trout in the river's currents see and eat more caddis, mayfly, and midges. Slough-cruisers often contain leeches, water boatmen, snails, and damselfly nymphs. It's like another fishing world along the same stretch of river.

Since many sloughs are shallow, clear, and weedy, cruising trout can be easy to see when they cross open water. Take up a camouflaged position, but one that allows backcasting room, and wait. If nothing is seen after a few minutes, sneak thirty feet or so down to another vantage point. Systematically look it over from beginning to end. Someone should be in residence. Trout will often fool you by being in the shallowest end, or by cruising out from under a weed bed when you've gotten too close and let your guard down.

Since the water is still and clear, trout get a good look at your offerings. Leaders seem agonizingly thick. All does not go your way. Be prepared to use very fine tippet and small nymphs or dries. Slough fish will often take surface or subsurface flies with equal suspicion. Don't overlook hoppers or Woolly Buggers either. I've cast the small stuff enough to chase the fish around the slough, only to have them take a hopper thereafter. Slough and big eddy cruisers are a sport in themselves.

Deep-Water Foam Lanes

Wherever serpentine foam lines ease across deeper pools and glides, hovering trout could be found. They look to this concentrated food

Deep, slow pools with foam lanes are home to many fish. They can be found rising, even after the hatch has waned. You can often see trout finning beneath the foam, and sometimes in schools. A dry fly with a nymph dropper is a good candidate, as they tend to hover close to the surface. Proceed with caution though, as all flat-water fish can see well.

source for meals, and perhaps overhead cover. Sometimes these fish rise heartily. Other times they can be spotted holding and cruising beneath the foam, rising now and then. This can be especially true when the sun is riding high.

Often it's a matter of unfocusing from bank waters, looking at the big picture, and constantly being aware of midstream potential. Routine focus shifts should be part of your trout-stalking game. Some deep-water foam line fish can be waded to, others are boat propositions.

Foam and scum line trout can school up, due to the abundance of available food. Bugs still litter the surface here long after the hatch itself has waned. Cripples, spinners, and assorted "leftovers" lay sodden in foam lines throughout the day. Some big slow-water foam lines can keep anglers busy for an hour, as their numerous trout rise, visibly cruise, and follow the ever-wandering foam trail. This foam doesn't chart a constant course. It swings from side to side, as eddies pulse and swirl. Trout travel with them so keep up with their changes.

Foam line and scum eddy trout sometimes take little notice of boats. They see so much floating around that they take the boat for scum too. This plays into the angler's hands since they can be approached within easy casting range. Pressured fish get nervous and aware of lines and leaders flashing overhead. Keep your false casts out of their view. Lead them by about six feet whenever possible. Sometimes circulating weeds and debris make this hard to do. If the fish are cruising, figure their probable path and let them swim to your fly, rather than dropping it on their head. In some very weedy eddies, dropping it just in front of them, but ever so lightly, is your only choice. Low-altitude, high-speed casts are less visible to fish than high, slow-motion ones, presuming you don't splash the line down. Shorten your line and false cast away from the fish first, making sure it's weed-free and in control. Trying to pick up all the line and casting it right back to the fish is a major error. Water droplets and weeds can fly everywhere, crashing down near or on the fish. Do everything right every time. This is guide experience talking.

Always give slow and deep-water foam lanes a good looking over. The shapes of finning, weaving trout are commonly found just beneath.

Hooking Subsurface Trout

Sight-nymphing is an exciting game. The stalk, cast, and "will he take it" anxiety are absorbing sport. When the trout is in clear view, watch for its mouth to open and close on your fly. It's usually best to set the hook as soon as you see or perceive that it's taken it, rather than waiting to feel the fish on. Once a trout takes the fly, it immediately realizes something is wrong and tries to blow it back out. Waiting to feel it can take too long and too late. Light tippet and small flies are less alarming, allowing fish to hold on longer before noticing the duplicity.

Sometimes fish will rush up to inspect a nymph at close range (especially in still water). Their opening and closing mouth can fool you as they breathe, making you think it's taken the fly. Your instinct to set the hook can scare the fish off by its unnatural motion. There are times when you just can't tell if the fish has taken or not. The best thing to do here is start a slow, swimming nymph retrieve. If the trout has taken it, you'll either see it shake its head and run off, or feel it. In either case, a tightening of the line is in immediate order. If the trout hasn't taken your fly, the natural swimming motion may solicit a strike, or at least a follow. This is less likely to scare the fish off than is the old bass-rod jerk. Expect your nerves to sabotage your best intentions at times. This is what sight-fishing is all about...visualization, action, emotion—and sometimes all goes awry!

In poor viewing situations, relying on a strike indicator is a better way to go. Shadows, clouds, wind, and low sun angles can make tracking subsurface trout difficult. They might only be visible on occasion. Slowly-stripped nymphs, leech patterns, or Buggers are also effective, hooking by feel.

One old Kiwi trick with slough and eddy cruisers goes as follows: Figure the trout's cruising path or "beat"; wait till it's going away and cast a weighted nymph, letting it sink into the silt that lines most slough bottoms; then twitch it up out of the mud as it approaches. The puff of mud often brings the trout rushing over to look. Sometimes they take it right away. Other times you're in the old "did he take it?" dilemma. In either case, it's good clean fun!

Sight-nymphing is almost as fun as catching rising fish. The stalking, rigging, and casts to get nymphs down to the trout's level all take some thought. Seeing them take and flee when the hook is set tops off this game.

Trout move into swifter runs to escape the heat of summer. Nymphs are more populous here too. Both sight-fishing and blind-casting are likely to produce results.

When sight-nymphing in a riffle, run, or glide, you may still be able to see the trout's mouth open and close. If fishing directly upstream, you might see the fish turn to one side to pick something up before facing back into the current. You can either go purely by sight, which is fun and builds sight-fishing skills, or use an indicator. There are times when an indicator drags the nymph around in an unnatural fashion. The non-indicator method is fraught with the same doubt and concerns as mentioned above, but with the benefit of the current carrying it on downstream and out of the fish's view if it hasn't taken it. A mistaken hookset here is less likely to spook it than it is in still water.

Using a dry fly for a strike indicator can be a productive sight-nymphing technique. The trout might go for either fly. Its occasional downfall is when the dry fly spooks the fish by landing or dragging just upstream from them. Another scenario is when the trout decides to go for the dry fly, and runs into the leader between the dry and the nymph. Sometimes this spooks them, sometimes it pulls the dry away just as they try to eat it, and sometimes they get snagged on the nymph, often in the side, back, or tail.

Sight-fishing beneath the surface takes dedication and practice. You need to cultivate your underwater vision through experience. It goes a long way in upgrading your trout education. You'll soon be catching fish where other people just walk by, and having great fun doing so. Every sight-fishing victory is a memory on file. Most every reach of clear water has a visible trout finning nearby.

Cutthroat trout, like western tanagers, are among the most beautiful creatures found in the Rockies. This western Montana specimen was caught on a dry fly after being spotted rising once. Early season stoneflies were the target. These can bring sporadic rises that anglers should put a memory lock on, then persue. Size 18-8 somber-colored stonefly species are prevalent on freestone rivers from late February till the high-water/snow melt period of mid May to June.

Chapter 5
Boat Stalking

Fish on! This fat rainbow was rising with some friends, and was boat stalked by a skilled caster. The boat was anchored in just the right position before the first presentation was made, using a downstream reach cast. Such team efforts produce a lot of fish across the West.

Float fishing is such a big slice of the western fishing pie that it deserves a closer look. The days of just floating down a lonely river with no one else on it, chucking Royal Wulffs has passed (though gloriously enough, this still works at times). Rivers are doing brisk business. Fish have become sophisticated. Equipment and techniques have evolved. There are float fishermen and then there are "boat stalkers."

Boat stalkers hunt rising and sighted fish while being highly mobile. Anchoring in a chosen position to allow the best presentation is critical (if wading isn't the best option). Fishing goes on between sighted fish with dry fly, nymph, and streamer, but the whole point of the trip—stalking fish—is never abandoned. Someone or everyone is always "looking," and not just at a strike indicator.

A boat allows you the convenience of having extra rods on board, rigged in various fashions. If there is just one angler in the bow plus a rower, the stern can hold an arsenal of extra rods, equipped in all manner of fish-catching arrangements. If both bow and stern fishermen are present, each can have one extra rod (comfortably), and thus four fishing approaches can be covered. The rower should be the primary fish hunter, though it helps if all are looking. Risers can be difficult to spot in riffles and in wobbling bank reflections.

Most fishermen are compelled to cast (though I do know some that won't cast until a rising fish is seen). This is how I would start the day if rising fish aren't obvious right out of the gate. I'd have the bow angler rig an indicator nymph or two, or dry-fly/nymph-dropper combination. I'd have the stern fisherman rig a streamer,

Woolly Bugger, or crayfish pattern. On one extra rod I'd tie up a match-the-hatch dry fly on a long, fine tippet. On the second extra rod I might put an easily visible and good floating match-the-hatch dry with an emerger dropper. (Naturally there'll be a lot of options, from midges to salmonflies.) Now we have rods rigged for most any situation.

Float fishermen look ahead to spot rising fish and plan their anchoring/casting strategy. Trout are rising in an eddy line and bank eddy. It's mid morning and the fish are rising best in what shadows remain. Expect the anchor to drag a bit before the boat comes to rest. If it drags too close to the fish, have the fisherman remain seated to cast. A downstream reach cast will do the trick here.

As the rower I would scan the river far and wide for risers, bulgers, insect concentrations, or any evidence of feeding fish. (Wind, currents, or micro-environments can cause concentrations of aquatic insects, thus increasing the likelihood of rising fish.) The anglers standing in the bow and stern have a better chance of spotting subsurface trout from their elevated positions. With the nymph on the bow rod and streamer at the stern, we test the fish's feeding mood for the day, at least until hatches bring them up. Some days, or hours of the day, they're laid-back feeders, not willing to go out of their way to eat. A nymph floundering by their nose has the best chance of success. Other days the barometer may be falling. There may have been no moon at night. A thunderstorm or wet front may be approaching. Fish can "turn on." In such conditions the streamer fisherman may do bang-up business. All the while, the rower looks for fish. The streamer fisherman can search for fish too once he makes his presentation. There's no need to watch a streamer as you fish it (though seeing a big fish come out to attack it is worthwhile). The more trout-hunting eyes the better.

While proceeding down the river, ever back rowing to slow the boat's pace, rising fish are sought. Expect to see them in edgewaters, in bank eddies and their leading edge riffle lines, in converging and secondary currents, up and downstream of midriver gravel bars and islands, and in "flats" of all descriptions. Anywhere off to the sides of the main current has promise. Trout like a comfortable push of water and food delivered to their nose. Any slowing flow and wandering foam lane should draw your eye. The slower the boat progresses the more you will see.

There's a big difference in this respect between a seasoned rower/trout-stalker, and a weekend "guest of honor" boatman (the kind you talk into rowing so you can fish). Having someone at the oars who doesn't know how to row, doesn't fish, and just wants to float the river and daydream will ruin your day's fishing! He won't slow down enough (back row all day) to effectively fish, and probably won't keep you within casting range of your targets. This gets very annoying.

A good rower will always back row and slow down (all day, every day), and always keeps you an appropriate distance from your targets. He knows when to row to a standstill and how early he needs to lower the anchor (not drop it) to come to a halt in a chosen spot. The aware rower becomes an extension of the fisherman. He senses the optimal casting distance and angle, and knows how close he can get to fish without spooking them. When boat stalking, both parties must be at the top of their games. While mistakes in both rowing and casting judgment are occasionally made, these are at least recognized and avoided as much as possible.

The Boat Stalking Approach

The big difference between a wade fisherman and a boat fisherman is in the angle of their approach. A wade-fisher usually stands in slower water near the shore and casts upstream into swifter flows. His line floats back towards him, creating slack. A boat angler is located in swifter water, casting into slower edgewaters and eddies. His line is instantly tightened and drug by the currents if he doesn't adapt to a different style. The same approach doesn't work for the boat fisherman. His main weapon and the cast that must be maximized to succeed is the downstream reach cast. The boat stalker doesn't cast

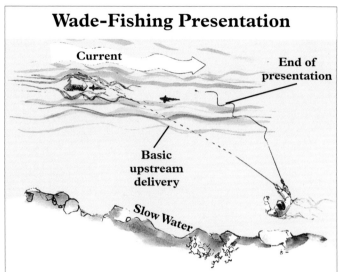

Wade-Fishing Presentation

In most wade-fishing situations the delivery is with a straight cast. The line slackens as it drifts back towards the wade fisherman. The angler casts from slow to fast water.

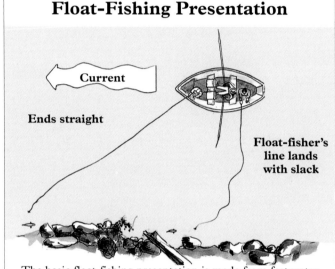

Float-Fishing Presentation

The basic float-fishing presentation is made from fast water into slow, and is cast at a slight downstream angle. The angler's line needs to land with slack on the presentation and the straighten as it approaches its target.

upstream in most situations, he casts downstream at a 45- to 60-degree angle. As the line shoots forward and downstream from his rod though, he smoothly "reaches" his rod and arm back upstream as far as he comfortably can, while the line is still in the air. When the fly lands downstream, his rod is pointing upstream on a fully extended arm, both held high. Now you can drop the rod and arm, following the fly's downstream progress with both. One quick mend at the beginning of this "follow" can prolong the drift without moving the fly, as it would later. The end of the presentation often finds the angler "reaching" downstream with body, arm, and rod, maximizing the drag-free drift. The feeding of slack is also part of the game. Shaking it out of the rod tip without dragging the fly becomes an art. By performing an extreme reach cast, following the fly with your rod tip, and doing a little mending and line feeding, you can get drag-free drifts of great length. This is the backbone, the heart and soul, the bread and butter, of the boat stalker's success (get the drift?).

Skilled float fishermen use downstream casts of about 45-60 degrees angled in towards shore, with a big "reach" at the end. This "pre-mending" operation allows much longer drag-free drifts of the fly. It goes against the grain of most small-stream fishermen's habits and prejudices. Relearning certain fishing skills is part of the float-fishing game.

The Reach Cast

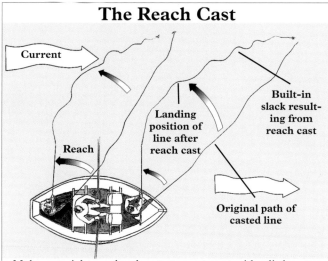

Current

Built-in slack resulting from reach cast

Landing position of line after reach cast

Reach

Original path of casted line

Make a straight overhead cast at your target with a little extra altitude and power. As your line begins to unfurl, reach your rod arm and rod upstream as far as you can, keeping the rod tip high. Drop the rod and line simultaneously. Mend as needed while following line on downstream with your rod tip as far as you can. Extra-long drag-free floats can be achieved with the reach cast. This only works when casting directly across or downstream. It doesn't work casting upstream.

Slack-Line Reach Cast

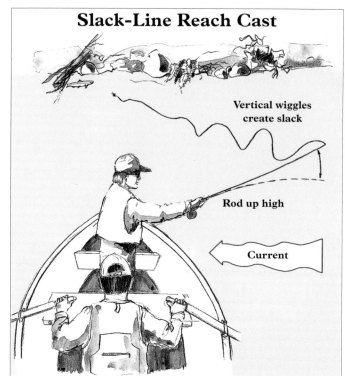

Vertical wiggles create slack

Rod up high

Current

A slack-line reach cast is made by wiggling the rod tip up and down vertically, while "reaching" with the rod upstream. This is done while the line is still in the air. The sooner you begin this vertical shaking after the forward casting stroke, and the more you wiggle the rod tip, the more slack will be built into your final presentation. As the fly is about to land, drop your rod tip and line to the water, and follow the line downstream with the rod tip.

It takes a little practice to perfect the reach cast. When you first try it, you tend to pull the fly back and away from its intended landing spot, even though the line should still be sliding through the rod guides as you "reach." You must actually cast more line than needed in the conventional sense. The angulation of the reach uses it up.

The downstream-angled reach cast is necessary to overcome the swifter water the boat is in, while allowing the fly a long drift in the much-slower water near the banks. A straight line cast (rod tip pointed at the fly) results in immediate line drag across the swifter water near the boat. Almost every cast should be a downstream reach cast!

This boat has anchored on some risers. Down-and-across slack-line presentations will soon be made. Pause just a second before setting the hook when casting downstream, allowing the fish to tilt back down, otherwise you can pull the fly right out of their unclosed mouth. The hook-up ratio is a little lower when casting downstream, but the trout-fooling rate can be higher, especially on flat water. Your fly is the first thing they see, not the leader.

Exceptions to this are when the boat is pulled over near the bank and you're casting upstream to rising fish as a wading angler would, if you're in the slow water of an inside bend casting out to a quicker midriver flow, and when casting across pond-sized eddies.

Not only does the downstream reach cast allow long drag-free drifts from a boat, it also places the fly out in front of the leader. It's the first thing the fish sees, and is more likely to fool twitchy trout.

Its weak point is that it's a less efficient hooking angle, since you're technically pulling the fly upstream and out of the fish's mouth. You make up for this by pausing half a second before setting the hook, allowing the fish to turn back down before tightening up. The bigger the fish, the slower they tend to rise and the more important this brief delay becomes. Some smaller and more eager trout make quick, rushing rises. A quicker hookset could be in order here.

The Boat's Position in Relation to Sighted Fish

Let's imagine we're approaching some rising fish near a boulder that's a few feet off the bank. We'll look at anchoring and presentation angles and how they effect the fishing. There is usually one, or perhaps two, specific anchoring locations in any given situation that will allow anglers the optimal chance for success. (In some cases, pulling over and wade fishing may be the best choice.) We'll discuss why certain boat positions work better than others. I might also add here that the boat is usually anchored for either the bow or stern caster's advantage. One boat position doesn't usually put both fisher-

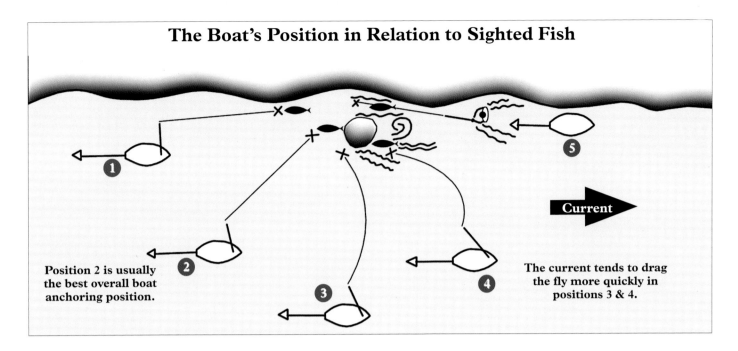

The Boat's Position in Relation to Sighted Fish

Position 2 is usually the best overall boat anchoring position.

Current

The current tends to drag the fly more quickly in positions 3 & 4.

men in an ideal casting location. Also, only one angler casts to any given fish, not both. The boat is positioned for whoever's turn it is. In any case, remember that some of the largest steady rising fish will be found in the slowest, shallowest edgewaters where they don't have to work against much current to feed. Choose your fly well!

Position 1

The more extreme upstream anchoring angle works best when there is a great deal of difference between the main current speed, and those of slower bank currents and eddies where trout are holding. An extreme downstream reach cast and close to the fish fly placement (three feet to just inches) can be necessary to get a drag-free drift over such fish. The extreme upstream anchoring angle can also be needed for fish that feed between a rock and the shoreline, a position in a secondary current that trout love.

The biggest problem with extreme downstream casts is that you have to pull your leader and fly back upstream past the fish to recast. Mend your line repeatedly out toward mid river first. This will help lead it away from the fish before pulling it in quietly and recasting. When casting almost straight downstream, you hope your first presentation or two does the trick. Spooky fish may not take more casts than that. Rest them between casts if they act the least bit nervous.

Pulling the boat over below, or downstream of such fish and casting up and over them could be a good option here, when conditions allow. Sometimes a deep bank, or thick willows that snag backcasts can make the wading approach more work than it needs to be. Using the boat to its full advantage as a mobile casting platform is the name of the game.

Position 2

The 45-degree down-and-across casting angle is the best overall boat stalking position, give or take a degree or two. A big body English reach cast is a necessity since the current the boat is in is swifter than the bank currents. Drop the fly 3-5 feet above the fish, closer in choppy or eddying water, a bit further in slick water where trout can see your cast in the air. Follow the line's downstream progress with your rod tip. Mending, and the feeding of line might also be needed to achieve the perfect drag free drift into your fish's mouth. Remember to pause half a second before setting the hook. Position 2 is the one I use most routinely when anchoring on fish.

Position 3

Being even with the fish makes presentations more difficult from a boat anchored in much current. It can be done, but the swifter current nearest the boat wants to whisk the fly away from the trout in short order. An extreme reach cast is needed here, dropped closer to the fish. Drag-free drift time won't be nearly as long as it was back in position 2. The stern angler will have the best chance, as he's the furthest upstream.

I usually end up at position 3 if my anchor drags excessively when aiming to stop at position 2. Occasionally, a last second sighting of a fish brings me to this anchoring location. In general, when rowing down the river, I like to look way ahead for rising fish, as well as closer at hand. In this way, I can plan my anchoring strategy. Before getting to the anchor lowering (not dropping) location, I back row strongly, bringing the boat to a standstill in the water, or even propelling it back upstream a bit. Now I lower the anchor quietly, for the sound of it hitting and dragging on the bottom can scare fish. The anchor will drag a bit (or a lot) depending on current speed, depth, and wind velocity and direction. If the trout spook from this operation, wait them out a while. In general, the heavier the hatch, the sooner they'll come back. (If they don't resume rising, try nymphing them before you leave. Trout usually resume feeding under water sooner than rising again.)

Position 4

This is usually a bad angle when boat stalking. Stronger currents near the boat tend to skid the fly away almost immediately. You might be able to get away with it in slower flows, or if fish are willing to chase down skittering caddis and such. (It is a good streamer angle.) A strong tuck cast helps prolong your fly's drift here.

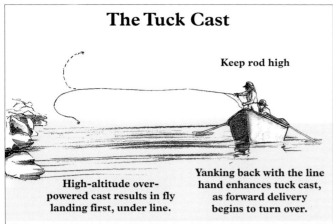

The Tuck Cast

Keep rod high

High-altitude over-powered cast results in fly landing first, under line.

Yanking back with the line hand enhances tuck cast, as forward delivery begins to turn over.

By overpowering a high-altitude cast and stopping it abruptly, the fly will "turn over" and then "under" the fly line. The fly will land first, allowing longer drifts in eddies, and helping nymphs sink deeper. Having your fly land before your line is always advantageous.

Again, I usually end up in this position by accident, due to anchor drag or last-second fish sightings. A strong tailwind is often the culprit. When combined with the current, there are times the boat just won't stop. A 30-pound anchor is the minimum for a drift boat. Thirty-five pounds is better. (More on anchoring safety later.)

Position 5.

If the upstream angles don't seem right, have failed, or if you've drug anchor below the fish, pulling in towards the bank and out of the current is your next approach. You can get out and wade, or if the willows are thick and tedious, anchor the boat just far enough out to clear the backcasts. Some guides will walk the boat bow first back upstream to the best casting position, especially if the wading or casting is tricky. Here you make the traditional "up-and-over" presentations. The choppier the water, the better your odds. Some educated flat-water fish can be tough customers. Any mistake can put them down. Try to make the first cast perfect.

The newer low-sided drift boats, like this Clackacraft 15-foot Low Profile, are superb fly fishing craft for moderate western rivers, where wind is a bigger rowing factor than rapids. In heavy water, higher-sided models and self-bailing rafts can be a better choice. Low-sided models are better to sneak up on fish with too, and easier to get in and out of. This angler has dismounted to cast to some trout rising in the morning fog.

Boat Options

And just what is the perfect fly fishing river boat? One that handles the water safely and is as inconspicuous as possible. Turbulent rivers favor well-rigged rafts, catamarans, or high-sided drift boats. Mellower rivers where wind can be a problem favor low-sided drift boats, prams, low-sided rafts, and catamarans. I'd stay away from bright colors and go for earth tones, grays, or even cammo. If you're in hot country, the heat-reflective qualities of a light-colored interior will be appreciated. The right length oars, an extra breakdown oar, life jackets, and a first-aid kit are a must. An anchor system and anchor of appropriate weight to stop the boat is also a must for serious boat stalking. Thirty pounds is a good starting point for drift boats and 12- to 15-foot rafts. You may need 35 or even 40 pounds in some rivers. Fast, deep currents and slippery, rounded stone bottoms don't stop a boat as well as shallow gravel ones do. I prefer inverted pyramid shaped anchors for overall bottom grabbing performance.

Anchoring Safety

You can't just drop anchor any old place. Boats are flipped or sunk stern first. Fishermen are drowned by boatmen who drop anchor in deep, fast water. Here's what happens. When an anchor is dropped in a deep, swift run, a lot of rope must be let out to stop it. The boat, if it holds, begins to swing from side to side on this long line, and sometimes wildly. Drift boats can get spun completely sideways, where the fast water catches and climbs the upstream gunwale. This can roll a drift boat over.

In a very heavy run, the anchor is likely to drag but should it get stuck between some boulders and jam, the back end of the boat can be pulled under water. Note that most drift boats have no floatation! A knife should be on board to cut anchor ropes in an emergency, when they're lodged in the bottom and can't be retrieved.

When anchoring in a moderately swift run (off to the side of the main current), the rower can stabilize the boat with his oars to keep it from swinging on the anchor rope. Hold them just under the surface, pointed downstream, with the oar blades positioned vertically. This dual front rudder effect will stabilize the boat to a large degree. I do this much of the time when anchored on rising fish. A boat swinging back and forth in the current is not a good

Stabilizing an Anchored Boat

Hold both oars in the water, parallel with the boat, with the blades positioned vertically. This double front ruddering effect will curtail a boat's swinging in the current when anchored.

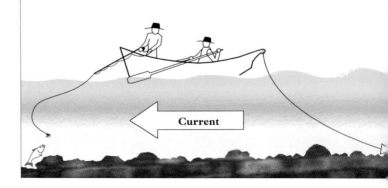

Current

One cannot anchor just anywhere. Heavy water and anchor-snagging bottoms should be avoided. If in doubt, don't drop it. Instead, just row the boat to a standstill while the anglers fish. Here, fishermen cover the converging currents at the end of an island while the guide rows them into place.

casting platform! The waves it makes can put fish down. Stabilize it with your oars.

When planning to drop the anchor, consider the following safety factors. Is it shallow enough, slow enough, and is the bottom structure of a nature that won't snag an anchor? Avoid deep, heavy runs, rapids, or bottoms with large chunky boulders or sunk logs. Choose moderate flows, even bottoms, and anchor out of the main force of the current. Row the boat to a standstill before lowering the anchor quietly. This allows the anchor to catch more easily and drag less. Make sure there is no danger just downstream from a spot you're thinking about anchoring in. The anchor could drag into it. If nothing else, it takes time to pull up the anchor when you leave, and there is a brief but decisive period when the boat is out of control. Give yourself a safe downstream buffer zone of open water below any anchoring position.

Anchor Hopping

Quite often the spot you first drop anchor isn't the best one for the angler's presentation. I usually plan to drop anchor just a little farther upstream than necessary in case the anchor drags more than anticipated. Then I plan to "anchor hop" to the best position, perhaps lifting and quickly re-dropping the anchor several times before getting there. At times you must restrain overanxious fishermen from casting till they're in perfect range. Many fishermen will try to jam a long, out-of-control cast to the fish while I'm still in the set-up stage. This can spook them by dragging the fly and leader over their heads. Have the chosen fisherman wait until the boat is in position and stabilized.

Anchor hopping has two facets, the current pushing the boat downstream, and the angle of the boat to the current when you briefly lift the anchor. Let's say you're a little too far out from the left bank (looking downstream), and still a bit too far upstream. First, shorten your anchor rope till it just holds the bottom. Next, back row with the right oar only. This spins the boat on the anchor rope till the stern is pointed 45 degrees towards the left bank. By

lifting the anchor now, water deflects off the right side of the angled boat, pushing it towards shore. A quick one second lift and re-drop will move you a number of feet closer to your goal, both downstream, and in towards shore.

It's necessary for the anchor rope to be short as possible when "anchor hopping," but not to the point where the boat starts dragging it downstream. Otherwise, it takes too long to pull it free. The 45 degree deflection or "ferrying" angle you achieved by rowing with the one oar will be lost. The boat will restraighten to the current and begin swinging before you can get a long rope in. Since it takes two hands to pull in the anchor, there can be almost no time lost between the prying oar strokes and the anchor hop. If you get the anchor rope tight enough that one hand can lift it free, then you can actually pry with the right oar hand, and lift the anchor just a few inches to clear the bottom with the left. (This is something I do to aim the boat out from shore when pulling the anchor free to go on down the river. The water deflects it in the direction you want to go.)

In tricky locations, it is possible to have the bow fisherman pull the anchor rope and re-drop it while the rower "pries" or rows the boat closer to the perfect position. Boat stalking is a team effort. Doing what it takes to master the situation can mean additional trout victories.

It may take several "hops" to get the boat in the ideal casting position, a little in, a little down, a little back out. (You can only go back upstream if the current isn't too strong for the rower to lift the anchor, overcome the downstream drift he loses while lifting it, and then row back above the position of his last anchor drop/drag.) I usually anchor for the bow caster. If it's the stern angler's turn, this requires a slight change of position, usually a little further downstream and out away from the target. Anchor hopping is a huge part of my daily guiding routine (except at the highest river flows), as many of our fish are "boat stalked."

At times the boat and anchor slide a little too close to the trout. In such cases, have the anglers remain seated. They're much less visible to the fish this way. You can typically approach fish more closely in lower sided craft with seated anglers, than you can in a high sided drift boat with standing ones. This can be a decided

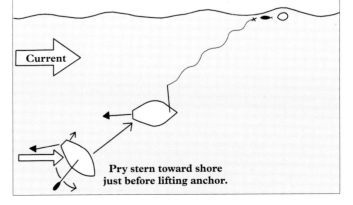

Anchor Hopping

By angling the stern in the direction you want to go, just before pulling the anchor, water will hit the side of the hull and deflect it in that direction. In this case, a one-second anchor hop drops the boat both downstream and in towards the shore a bit. The anchor rope must be as short as possible when doing this.

Current

Pry stern toward shore just before lifting anchor.

Whenever you find yourself too close to trout, remain seated while casting. Trout can easily see tall figures waving rods when close by.

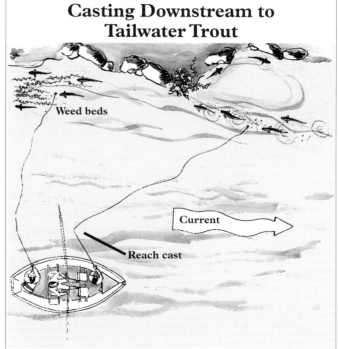

Casting Downstream to Tailwater Trout

Weed beds

Current

Reach cast

Anglers use the reach cast to achieve a "fly-first," drag-free presentation. The bow angler is casting to a school of trout feeding in an eddy line. The stern angler is casting to fish scattered across a weedbed flats.

advantage, especially if the trout are extra wary, or if your anglers can't cast far with total control. On the other side of the coin...many experienced float fishermen prefer to cast while standing, from the comfort of knee braces. They have the skill to fish long lines on big reach casts, dropping even Tricos at 60 plus feet. To each, his own...but if you find yourself too close to fish, remain seated. I've see many, many a fish spook when a boat angler stands to cast.

There are many locations where boat anglers can pull over and wade to rising fish. This is the best way to go at times. One thing I notice with some fish of my routine acquaintance, is that they seem used to being approached by bank fishermen and seem to spook more easily from that approach. Many of their natural enemies—kingfishers, heron, mink, and such—are also bank-based predators. Therefore, trout can have a love/hate relationship with banks, and are forever on guard. Just by casting to certain fish from the mid-river angle seems to up their catchability. There are many places I prefer to boat stalk trout from the outside, rather than dismounting to wade fish them from the inside. This of course takes experience with particular fish. On the whole though, the outside approach (from mid-river casting to banks), is an effective one.

Float fishing was once equated with drifting all day and throwing large attractor dry flies, streamers, or monstrous nymphs. While these tactics work well at certain times and

places, the game has come a long way from there. A 6X and the latest PMD emerger might be employed while anchored half an hour on fish. Binoculars might be carried to spot protruding noses. And of course, any small nymph with a bead at the head has a great chance of being eaten (even when cast to risers). The latest boat and tackle technology and fly evolution aren't lost on boat stalkers. They're at the top of their game, trying new angles and approaches in the most thoughtful manner. There are hidden grooves of fish in the river to be discovered, and new ways to dupe the ones everybody knows about. From size 4 Salmonflies to size 24 midge emergers, the boat stalker is ready to take on the river world!

Releasing a large brown to keep the big-fish gene pool going strong. Every brown has different spot patterning, colors, and looks. Each is beautiful to behold, a true resident of the cobbled streambed.

Chapter 6
Seasons, Hatches And Flies For Trout-Stalking Success

An angler gets good action from an autumn Baetis *mayfly hatch. Though the bugs hatch and the fish rise much better on overcast, rainy, and snowy days during this hatch, some are still to be found on sunny days.*

Trout can be stalked year round in the Rocky Mountain west. Let's take a quick seasonal overview, starting in late winter. Tailwater rivers, ice-free sections of freestoners, and spring creeks might all reveal midge sipping trout now, but very little else. The occasional splash to a little winter stonefly might be seen in mountain streams. Early *Baetis* mayfly hatches could be seen on spring creeks. In winter and early spring's clear water, trout may be seen beneath the surface and sight nymphed, even though the angle of the sun is still low. This becomes especially true as rainbows start staging to spawn. Blind fishing small nymphs and slow streamers is always an option. Egg patterns and pink scuds work well at this time, as do cressbugs, whose real-life counterparts stay active in cold river waters. A variety of midge dries, emergers, and larva should be standard equipment, along with small parachutes for indicator flies, fine tippet, weights, and indicators.

Come spring, various hatches start popping, with midges still a mainstay. Late morning through early evening is the time to look for them. First are the size 16-18 *Baetis* mayflies or "olives," a consistent spring and fall hatch that trout love. Next comes Western March browns, a slightly larger, size 16-14 mottled wing dun. Size 14-16 grannom caddis boom out in some places, beginning the season's progression of caddis hatches. Overcast, drizzly, or snowy days show more bugs and rising fish in most cases, except with the warmth-loving spring stoneflies. Trout too are sun shy in spring, much preferring overcast conditions in which to rise.

Spring stoneflies carry over from late winter. The first ones are small as size 20s. Size 16-18 is a good working size. Various species become larger as spring progresses, up to size 8s. (The giant salmonflies, and golden stones come in early summer's high-water

These midge larvae and adults were pumped from a February trout's stomach on a tailwater river. This is common trout fare, and can also include cress bugs, immature mayfly nymphs, the odd crayfish, and even plankton and Daphnia *or water fleas.*

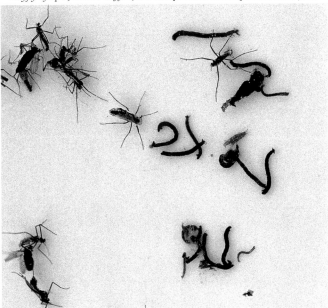

Baetis *mayfly duns begin popping as early as March in some places, and definitely by late April. It's a dominant afternoon hatch that trout love. On damp and overcast days, the hatch can be very profuse, with the duns too cold to take off. Thousands of them riding the currents can bring up a lot of steadily rising trout. Size 14-20 patterns match this hatch, depending on the water type.*

A variety of stoneflies hatch from February till high water. The first ones are small (size 16-20) and black or dark brown. From March to May, size 14-8 species appear. These range from black to medium grays and olive brown. It's common for several species to be around at the same time in a scattered fashion. Rises to them are sporadic, as is their availability to fish on the surface.

period.) The early versions are black or dark brown. They lighten in color as the world warms, assuming shades of olive/brown and gray, with lighter-toned undersides. Sunshine and warmth activate these species. They can be seen helicoptering about spring mountain rivers this way and that, largely on warm afternoons. The occasional splash of a trout rushing to take one should be target locked in your eyes at once, and apprehended. Steady sippers aren't the rule here. An assortment of small Stimulators, Trudes, and even dark caddis patterns, size 18-6 cover this action. They make good strike indicators as well.

Sometime in late spring/early summer snow starts melting and rivers rise. Muddy water can ruin stalking for long periods. Each drainage varies. Most tailwater rivers and spring creeks remain

clear, but even they can rise. You may have to hunt down the clear water, rising fish hotspots.

Lakes become a prime option now, just as soon as the ice goes off them. Big rainbows are targeted, patrolling lake shores in search of spawning sites. Huge 'bows can be sight-fished in the right locales. Midge and *Callibaetis* mayfly hatches bring lake fish up, as do some caddis species including the big "traveler sedge." This size 6-10 lake caddis runs across the surface to shore after hatching, bringing slashing takes from trout.

Western March browns start just after the Baetis *on a seasonal time frame, and overlap with the hatch. They are a late-morning to early-afternoon hatch generally, in the size 14-16 range.*

Stimulators and other downwing patterns fool a lot of stonefly-conscious trout. This trout took a big one during salmonfly season (mid-May to mid-July depending on elevation). Smaller, darker versions work better earlier in the year, from March to May. These patterns continue working as waters drop in July and on into early August, when most stonefly species give out for the season. Golden stoneflies, and the smaller olive, green, brown, and yellow species, are prominent post run-off hatches on swift freestone rivers.

Callibaetis mayflies are prominent lake hatches. They also occur in slow, weedy stretches of river. Mid to late morning is the time frame. Both duns and spinners can be on the water. Note the fly's speckled body and patterned wings. Callibaetis nymphs are active swimmers and are found on lake trout's menus, along with scuds, midge pupae, and damselfly nymphs.

Pale morning dun mayflies greet summer anglers across the west. Typical hatch time is late morning, from mid-June to late July. In some places, evening occurrences are common as well. Size 16-20 dry flies, emergers, cripples, spinners, and nymph patterns have evolved to match this sometimes demanding hatch. Trout can get very picky when focused on the emergers. Go prepared with a variety of patterns.

Prime time in the summer is when rivers first drop and clear. (This could be any time from late June to mid July depending on location and yearly snow pack.) Just prior to this, salmonflies and golden stoneflies hatch, bringing a crowd of anglers and mixed success. Salmonflies tend to hatch at high-water periods, but golden stones can coincide with the dropping and clearing period—a great treat if you hit them right. It's always worth an expeditionary try though. Big fish on size 4 dries aren't an everyday affair. Every big swirl seen should be worked over well, as should edgewaters in general. Big stonefly nymphs fished under an indicator are standard equipment on freestone rivers should the dries be ignored.

Now that waters have dropped, all kinds of notable hatches occur. Golden stoneflies could be going strong if you're lucky. This can be a major surface treat, with fish slamming size 4-8 Stimulators and such. The big dry/nymph combo can be very productive now. Size 16-18 pale morning dun mayflies are widespread and important to match in every stage. You might get away with size 14s on backcountry rivers. More realistic sizes and patterns will be needed to fool the educated trout of spring creeks and dam-controlled rivers. A myriad of caddis species from size 14-20 pop too, with cinnamon and green bodies being most prevalent. Some size 14-16 fast-water mayflies can be seen on freestone rivers. These don't

The giant size 4 salmonfly is a legend on western waters. It hatches in high-water periods on many rivers, making the fishing a "hit or miss" proposition. When you hit it right, memorable days are had. Banging big dries and nymphs along banks, where the insect activity is focused, is the name of the game.

The stomach pump tells all...in this case, the trout had been eating both spent caddis adults and caddis emergers (lower right corner of photo). The little and numerous green items are Daphnia, or water fleas. Presumably, these wash over the dam from the lake above the tailwater river in which this fish lives. These are the numerically dominant food item in many tailwater trout stomachs.

Western lakes produce big pre-spawning trout as soon as the ice goes off in spring. When rivers rise and flood in June, lakes become prime stalking grounds. Callibaetis and midge hatches bring fish to the surface, while others can be spotted subsurface cruising lake edges and flats.

PMD and Trico spinners are big-time food items on many western rivers. Female PMD spinners are a pale yellowish green, while the males are reddish tan to brown. Both are size 18s or so. Black and olive Trico spinners are size 20-24s. When on the water in great numbers, trout will slide off to the slowest currents to sip in the deceased. Eddy lines, bank edges, backwaters, and flats can all show steady risers. Spent-wing patterns should be on hand, in sizes 16-22. Pale olive, rusty, and black are good color standbys. Morning and evening are prime spent-wing times, but fish can be sipping them throughout the day.

ride the surface as long as PMDs. Soft Hackle mayfly emergers fished just under the surface can be more productive. Medium to small stoneflies in an assortment of colors and tones, from size 8-16 add to the mix. Some are duller browns, tans, and olives. Others are small and bright greens and yellows. The whole early summer world is beautifully colored, alive and full of action. Aquatic insects fly in every direction, each hovering over its favorite water type. It's a time of plenty, where attractor patterns like Stimulators, Trudes, Parachutes and Wulffs can work wonders.

In places, the big mayflies might be found come early summer—size 10-12 green and brown drakes. Such hatches can be very localized or spotty. It's the more profuse hatches of smaller flies like *Baetis*, PMDs, caddis, and midges that tend to bring the steadiest fish to the surface for the longest periods. Early summer hatches can occur almost the whole day, especially if it's overcast, with a little light rain. These are days to savor. Cover all your hatch bases, with an extra emphasis on the smaller size size 16-20 species. Research your chosen fishing location to learn its particular idiosyncrasies. Each river's hatches, fish behavior, and fishing demands vary somewhat.

As summer progresses, mountains brown, and waters drop and warm and trout get pickier. They've been fished to repeatedly now, and they see well in the low, clear flows. Hatch activity drops off a bit, and becomes less diverse. Aquatic insect species, with some exceptions, get smaller in size, but can be very profuse in number. "Trico" mayflies dominate morning action. Their huge mating swarms that parallel rivers banks and nearby roads (which look like rivers to them), appear as smoke over the river. Their tiny

size 22 spent wings can coat the water, feeding picky fish. Schools of trout may gang up on the action in eddy lines, foam lanes and pools. PMDs have already or are beginning to fade but caddis are still at large.

Hatches become more of a morning or evening affair now. Terrestrial insects (along with "leftover" Trico spinners and such) fill the midday bill. Hoppers, ants and beetles are classic summer producers when warm afternoon breezes blow thunderheads across blue mountain skies. Small size 16-20 Parachute Adams, Royal Wulffs and Renegades can do well too, when targeted to part-time

These flying ants, plus some caddis adults and emergers, were pumped from a July trout's stomach. This was not along a bank as you might expect, but from a mid-river riffle about 80 feet from shore. Flying ant patterns in sizes 14-20 are always good standbys when waters are low. I've found fish eating ants from April through September, and in various locations and water types.

Early to mid summer, just after rivers drop from high water, is prime rising fish time on most Rocky Mountain rivers.
This angler checks the hatches on a big dam-controlled river. Fish populations and sight-fishing challenges are numerous in tailwater rivers across the West.

Trico spinners swarm over river banks prior to mating and egg-laying. Shortly after these smoke-like clouds are seen, thousands of tiny spinners will coat the river's surface. This fly glut can bring up most of a river or stream's trout.

Most anglers can't wait till hopper time. Just when the hatches are waning and the trout are getting picky, along come hoppers to liven things up. They make great strike indicators too, with small beadheads trailing beneath. Big fish like hoppers, anglers who keep banging away with them are usually rewarded.

Streamside spider webs can clue you in as to what the trout might be taking. Trico spinners, midges, and the odd caddis are present in this one, as they are in resident trout stomachs.

sippers. The hopper/nymph dropper is an excellent summer combination, and a great way to pass the time between sighted fish. Some big trout go for hoppers if you keep them on the water!

In lakes, damselfly dries and nymphs add to the action. These fish can get into hoppers too. *Callibaetis* and Trico mayflies, caddis, and midges keep lake trout looking up. "Gulpers" are found in places, trout that cruise and gulp in quantities of spent insects come mid to late morning. This is the lake equivalent of trout schooling to eat Tricos.

Late summer, the latter half of August through mid-September, shows a slow down in many fishing locales. The water is at it's warmest, the fish are at their most lethargic, and many hatches are waning. Get out at dawn to look for risers before the sun hits the water. Hopper/dropper your way through the day, always keeping an eye out for sipping fish. Sight nymphing can be an amusing option now, with the sun at your back for best viewing. Evening should show an increase in rising activity, but sometimes not till

just before dark. Size 24 tiny blue-wing olives, size 18-16 small western red quill spinners, size 16-20 caddis and midges are likely players. Your expectations should be lower at this time of year, with the exception of some high-elevation fisheries, cold tailwaters and spring creeks.

As soon as it begins cooling off in the fall, and especially in the first cold rain or snow showers, trout activity picks up. They start taking indicator nymphs more freely. Fall hatches get their attention. The size 24 tiny olives of late summer are replaced by the larger size 20-18 *Baetis* mayflies. This is autumn's best all-around hatch. Size 16s and even 14s can work in riffle lines, as trout seem to become a little easier to fool come autumn. Caddis and midges continue, including the giant October caddis. This size 6-8 rust-bodied, gray-winged beast can bring up big fish on rivers across the west, including steelhead. October caddis dries like the Goddard and Stimulator variations make great strike indicators too, replacing or augmenting hoppers. Big boils down river should bring visual locks, noting exact casting locations.

Callibaetis (pictured here) and Trico spinners bring up "gulpers" on lakes. These fish cruise and avidly rise to spent mayflies and midges. "Gulpers" are a mid- to late-morning institution on a variety of lakes (and rivers) across the West, especially in late July and August.

Fall Baetis mayfly hatches give great sport. Overcast, rainy and snowy days are best, showing the most bugs and rising fish. From noon till dark is when dry-fly anglers need to get on stream. This hatch carries well into November in many places.

This size 16 mahogany dun sports the gray wings found on many spring and fall mayflies. Dark colors absorb heat, making their chilled hatching seasons more comfortable. Summer mayflies tend to be lighter in color, to reflect heat. PMDs are prime examples of this.

Midges accumulate on the side of a winter drift boat. Indicator nymphing and some sight-fishing to risers provide good sport.

Other fall hatches include size 16 mahogany duns and the size 12 "white fly." Both are sideline affairs unless you're in the right place and time. (Again, each river flows to its own seasonal hatch rhythm.) Mahogany duns are edgewater migrating mayflies, many crawling out onto rocks to hatch. The "white fly" *Ephoron* is a twilight-only hatch on silt/gravel-bed rivers of a slower nature. It's a big hatch in a very limited time frame and place. Few anglers experience this natural wonder in the west (it's also a big eastern hatch).

Fall fish are "happy fish," willing to eat and give good sport. Water temperatures are right, hatches are lessening, and they must put on condition for the winter and upcoming spawn. It's a great time of year to fish, though not so prolific as when rivers first drop and clear for the summer, back in late June and July.

Many western rivers continue to fish very well through November and into December. Hatches are few, mostly midges and some *Baetis*, but the rising fish can be many. Streamers,

Dry-fly fishing lasts later into the year than many fishermen realize. Here in central Montana, November is a premium month. Most of December is good too, though the best action becomes more localized. Routinely, cold weather doesn't generally knock off the dry-fly fishing till around Christmas. Even after that, midging trout can be found.

sometimes slow or even dead drifted, work well now, as food choices are really dropping off. Blind fishing consumes greater portions of the day. Nymphing can be excellent. As in much of fishing, high-pressure sunny days are not likely to be as productive as low-pressure overcast and humid ones. Hours when the fish are "on" are shorter, as are hours of daylight to fish. Nonetheless, some of my most productive days of the year have come in November.

The first Arctic subzero fronts are what really shuts down the sight fishing. These aren't usually routine until late December-February. Less and less fish rise after each front, though daytime temperatures can get back up into the 40s between them. The lower sun angle makes sight nymphing difficult too. It's indicator nymph or streamer time when it's warm enough to fish (more often than many people think). Midging trout on the surface are bonus fish (except on some tailwaters and spring creeks). Beadheads, Pink Scuds, Cressbugs, egg patterns, and midge larvae win the day now, fished deep, slow and systematically.

Cressbugs remain active in cold water and are a favorite of spring creek and tailwater trout. Size 10-16 imitations fished along the bottom are routine producers. Hanging a smaller midge larva pattern off this is a common tailwater practice, fished beneath a strike indicator.

Fishing Gear

When it comes to rods, the choices are endless. Modern graphite models are superb, though pricey. Since most rod companies have jumped on the "free replacement" bandwagon for competition purposes, I guess we're now paying for two or three rods at the time of the initial purchase. Some are still on the brittle side and can break with the least amount of abuse. Word of mouth from longtime users and honest retailers can help point you in the right direction. Baby an expensive rod, in any case. Some less-expensive rod makers offer very serviceable products too. Instead of paying a couple hundred dollars more for the latest "generation" graphite, a frugal angler could buy a moderately priced rod that's one-line weight heavier and gain some of that rigidity they're looking for. That is to say, he could buy a less-expensive 6-weight rod instead of a pricey 5-weight one, and fish a variety of line weights on it. The rod will weigh a little more, but hey, you can get stronger!

Considering the prevalent winds that greet you in the Rocky Mountain west, I'd rather go a little overgunned than undergunned, if carrying only one rod. My favorite all-purpose rod (at the moment) is an 8 1/2-foot 6-weight (it's actually about 8'4" since I broke a bit of the tip cleanly off). It cuts through the wind better than a more air-resistant 9-foot rod does, and can punch either hoppers or Tricos across a breeze.

Most western anglers prefer 9-foot 4- to 6-weight rods for general work. Nine-foot rods are safer than short ones when fishing from a boat too. You hook your companions less often. Shorter, lighter rods are great fun when you're besieged by calm air and close in on rising fish. Seven- or even 8-weight rods are good for routinely chucking big stonefly nymphs, streamers, salmonfly dries and hoppers.

Weight-forward floating fly lines are tops for all-around dry fly, nymph and shallow streamer fishing. Some anglers prefer double tapers for close-in, delicate dry-fly work (others use weight-forwards with extra-long leaders). Sink-tip fly lines are great for punching out streamers while float fishing and streamering shallower rivers and lake edges. Full-sinking lines of various densities allow you to cover deeper lake waters and big, heavy river runs.

I generally start with a 9-foot leader and add tippet to that. On clear, flat water where trout twitch at their own shadow, 12-foot-plus leaders can be a good idea. On broken freestone rivers, and especially when the fish are really "on," a 7-foot overall leader can be plenty. Your casting distances can be shorter here and this turns over easily.

We commonly use 2-4X tippet for a lot of rocky freestone work, and 2-6X tippet in the educated/flat-water trout realm. There are certainly cases where going lighter than this ups your odds. We even use 2X for hopper fishing, especially if they're models (like the Parachute Hopper) that tend to spin and twist your line. Even flat-water trout will take them on 2X if they're really looking. Murky water salmonfly fish have even less problem with this. I use 3-4X for medium-sized dries (8-14), from Golden Stones, Stimulators, and small hoppers on to large attractor patterns and October Caddis. Check the tippet often for frays, knots, and weak spots. If dropping a nymph off one of these, 4X is a good choice. This makes a two-fly leader system

Match your tippet to the job at hand. A 6X did the job on this fish, a flat-water rainbow sipping PMDs. The same fish might have taken a beadhead nymph on 4X, and later in the season, a hopper on 3X. I'd use nothing less than that for streamers, often going to 2X.

A school of trout, at least twenty, rises along an inside bend. This calm flat was peppered with Baetis *and midges on a November afternoon. A size 16 Parachute Adams on 5X fooled several of these fish. Earlier in the summer, 6X and a smaller fly would have been a better choice. The sun was higher then, and tippets cast bold shadows. Come fall, trout become a bit easier to fool.*

that still turns over reasonably well. The lighter tippet to the nymph allows it to sink more easily in the currents. If constant snags are part of the game, go up to 3X.

For medium/small flies (size 12-16), I'd still use 4X on broken water if the fish let me get away with it, mostly to battle leader abrasion when a trout runs it along the rocky streambed. On mellower gravel-bottomed rivers where trout can see better, I'd go right to 5X, perhaps using a tippet as long as three feet.

For small (size 16-24) flies and picky fish, 6X is a good starting point. Tippet material is getting stronger per diameter as the decades roll by. Long tippets of 2 to 4 feet can be more productive than shorter ones at times, as they allow better drag-free drifts across oscillating surface currents, particularly those made by waving subsurface weed beds. Long tippets also stretch more, acting as a shock absorber with beefy trout specimens. Try 7X if trout routinely "duck" every presentation, and try "leader sink" too. (There's a big difference between a trout refusing a pattern after inspection and a trout that "ducks" every presentation that goes by. Here, they go down before it even gets to them and wait for it to pass overhead before resuming their rising gait.)

Some anglers prefer to sneak right up behind trout as closely as possible, working quick, precise casts up and over their heads. What I'll sometimes do with a steady rising trout, in an attempt not to spook it, goes as follows. After slowly and cautiously moving up to an ideal casting position below, I'll work out a high-speed series of false casts off to the side of the trout, so it can't see in the air (one of the easiest ways to spook fish). Ultra high-speed, low casts are more difficult for them to see than high-altitude, slow, flopping ones. I'll watch (figuring out it's rise rhythm) while continuously false casting. Then I wait for it to rise one time and make a quick up-and-over cast while the rings of it's riseform are still spreading. In this way, it's water disturbance helps mask my cast. I try to drop the fly just far enough upstream to match the trout's rise rhythm.

At other times the down-and-across reach cast fools more fish, with some line-feeding often necessary. (Described in Chapter 5.) Experiment with different approaches. Each fish and location can

offer a different challenge. Upstream, across, down, sun at your back, to the side, what have you. You might improve your view of fish, fly, and contrasting background, and achieve the best casting angle all in one move. The ideal positioning can add up to more fish caught, especially with the demanding ones.

Staying low and getting closer to targeted fish improves most fishermen's casting accuracy. Having spent many years on Montana's Missouri–a big, wide, yet smooth-flowing river–I'm more comfortable with medium casting distances of 40-50 feet, and much of it down and across. Anglers not used to big, even water have a more difficult time perceiving the exact, "on a dime" drift lane at longer distances. This kind of adjustment takes practice to perfect. But back to the rigging...

My favored knots are blood or barrel knots in the upper, thick part of the leader, for their less bulky diameter. I like the triple surgeon's knot for the tippet, for its greater strength. To tie on the fly, I go with a Trilene knot (as in Trilene Line Co.), this is just like an improved clinch knot except that the tippet goes through the eye of the fly twice at the onset of the knot, instead of once. Everything else is the same. This through-the-eye-twice move spreads the line stress around the eye better, taking it from a 80-90% breaking strength

Extreme Downstream Casts

Extreme downstream casts are used when casting to sighted rising fish that can't be stalked from below. By hugging the bank with the boat, the angler is kept out of the heavy midriver flows that would make exacting drag-free drifts of a fly difficult. This is a "bow only" presentation. The stern angler reels in and sits out of the action. If a number of bank-huggers occur in such situations, the anglers can switch positions in the boat. Such fish often require repeated casts, finesse, and good slack-line reach cast presentations.

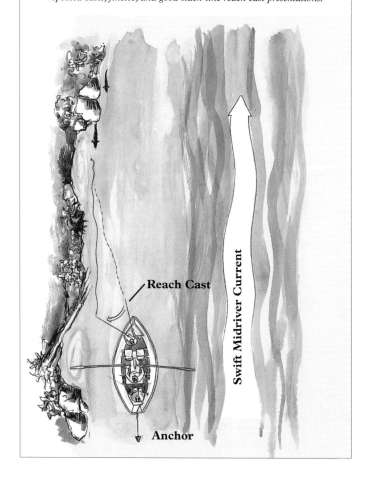

Black Wing Parachutes are easier to see when viewed against gray and open sky glare. This is often the case when wade fishing larger western rivers. Trout like the bold wing silhouette too, especially when gray-winged mayflies are hatching, spring and fall. Black wings are great for twilight fishing situations as well, unless you're facing a dark bank reflection. This size 16 Black Wing Parachute Pheasant Tail is an excellent pattern, both here and abroad. Black-wing caddis variations are good to have on hand, as are Black-wing Parachute midges. I tie white- and black-wing Parachutes to meet different background viewing conditions.

knot to an almost 100% knot. (It has been written up as a 100% knot in several places.) Few trout fishermen seem to be aware of the Trilene Knot. When using it, the tippet knot usually gives before the knot to the fly. Your overall leader-to-fly strength is definitely bumped up a notch. This can be especially important with tiny flies, where any weakness (or abrasion) can end the game. Check your leader for frays after every encounter, whether it's with a toothy brown trout or a streamside rock or branch.

Knowing the hatches beforehand, and coming prepared with a good variety of flies, will up your chances for the day. This fine trout was rising in a shallow, coverless edgewater. Spent caddis were his preference, a well-delivered reach cast his downfall.

Chapter 7
The West & Beyond

A fisherman works on a big New Zealand trout below a riffle drop-off. Dozens of clear rivers, stunning scenery, and fish averaging 23 inches– it's a trout-stalker's wonderland. Twenty-six-inchers aren't uncommon and many will take dry flies. OK, so they're sparse in number and take some walking and looking to find. It's not for everybody, but the true trout-stalker can have exquisite experiences here.

Trout-stalking has almost unlimited possibilities across the west. Big-name rivers and hushed tributaries both offer the observant angler great sport. The clear Rocky Mountain waters of late winter/early spring open the door. High run-off water from snow melt fouls up many places for extended periods, but lakes, spring creeks and dam-controlled rivers can take up this slack come early summer. Small feeder streams clear first and can make great stalking grounds. The fish can be easy to see, even when not rising in smaller waters. These too have their own hatch regimen, which can include stoneflies, PMDs and the like. Summer options abound most everywhere, as hatches bring up rising fish, and the high sun angle illuminates nymphing ones. The light and hatches drop off a bit by autumn, but opportunities are still ripe in most quarters. Rivers are at their lowest levels and the trout want to eat.

Besides trout, salmon and steelhead can be seen, at least for those that hunt them. Pike and bass are seen in lakes. Even carp are sight-fished for in places, and can rise to dry flies. It's training of the eye and setting the mind to hunt fish that opens new doors. Resist the urge to cast, for just a moment. Look before you leap. Your possibilities can be expanded in familiar settings.

For instance, a trophy-trout lake can have big pre-spawners cruising the shores after ice out. Only those that hunt them at the time catch them. Come summer they'll be gulping Trico and *Callibaetis* spinners in the morning and cruising in search of damselfly nymphs and scuds later in the day. Twilight will bring them to the top again, even if just for the larger midges that lakes support. By learning the seasonal possibilities and polishing your fish-spotting skills, many new stalking opportunities open up in your own backyard.

One December I was float-fishing near my Montana home, the fishing was good and varied. A friend sight-fished for, among others, a 21-inch rising brown trout in six inches of water with a size

Day in and day out, nymphs like this PMD are a trout's primary food source. Sight-nymphing is an exciting game.

High-altitude lakes become good fishing options when rivers are high—if you can get to them. Heavy snowpack years make the going tough till most of it melts off your hiking route. Drive-to lakes are always an option when rivers are blown.

16 Parachute Adams. Many fish were seen rising to midges and the odd *Beatis*. Great dry-fly fishing for Christmas! One can often stretch the fish-stalking season farther than you might have realized was possible by just getting out and looking.

Big New Zealand trout have limited food options, especially on South Island rivers. Insects make up the bulk of their diet, but even these are sparse compared to some of our rivers. The result is 3- to 10-pound trout that will sip mayflies. Nothing wrong with that! This big one took a dry fly on a small, secret river. Most serious Kiwi anglers won't tell you where the best places are. There are few fish and premium spots provide rare sport.

Many anglers I know, fanatics to be sure, honed their trout-stalking skills in New Zealand. Where, stalking before wetting a line is a way of life. The water is clear as air. Trout average very close to 23 inches. Twenty- to 30-inch trout dominate the many scenic headwater rivers. There are dozens and dozens of these streams. The trout's food choices are limited however. Even double-digit fish sip the sparse hatches of mayflies. The river valleys are among the world's most beautiful. What's not to like?

To tell you the truth, trout populations are very low in most New Zealand rivers, as are overall catch rates. Averaging 2 or 3 good fish a day is considered fine work. It's not Alaska, and no place for the impatient or those who can't walk miles of rocky riverbed a day (and then turn around and walk back). The overall stalking aesthetic is so high though, that those of the right hunter's spirit are enchanted with both the land and its fishing.

Small crystalline, jade-hued rivers flow wild through golden tussock meadows, green beech forests, and rocky crags that soar above the tree line, where the snow may never melt. Fantails flit in streamside bushes, paradise ducks fly on upstream, while a 24-inch trout weaves in two feet of clear, faceted water. Your cautious stalk, a bushy dry fly, the slow-motion take...it's all so visual! New Zealand memories can last a lifetime.

Risers, nymphers, lake edge and slough cruisers, it's all here, and has been in New Zealand since the 1870s. The fishing, fishing history and traditions are most interesting. British styles mix with American ways, but the no-nonsense Kiwi angler has his own methods, his own hatches and strategies. Strong legs, a long "bush

Fish on! Many New Zealand trout like green-bodied Humpies, as green "manuka beetles" are common along mountain rivers. Smaller, shallow rivers like this one provide the best and most enjoyable opportunities. Trout in this river average 22 to 28 inches. Small trout seem to migrate downstream to big, mainstem rivers, lakes, and to ocean estuaries to grow up. All the fish in most headwater rivers are big. This, among other things, is what makes New Zealand so different.

walk," cunning eyes and a true cast...it's a different world for most Yankee fly-fishers.

Sight-fishing in the ocean is gaining in popularity. There's a lot more ocean, bay and estuary than quality river mileage. Bonefish, permit, tarpon and sailfish are of course well known. The Bahamas, Christmas Island, Mexico and Central America, even the Indian Ocean...exotic destinations quickly come to mind. Other dynamic fish species like giant trevally, black tip sharks, and even marlin beckon those that seek truly aggressive fish.

This kind of fishing costs real money, especially for the long-time trout fisherman. New rods and reels (and they do not come cheap), big boats, travel expenses and guides keep this kind of fishing out of reach for many anglers, except perhaps for the odd indulgence.

There are saltwater fisheries though where trout fishermen can get by with the gear they might already have, using craft as small as kayaks, canoes and jon boats. Inshore estuaries around the country are teeming with life and opportunities for fishing excitement. Barrier islands and shallow water keep waves down, making small boating safe when conditions are right. Stripers and bluefish dominate the Northeast coastal fisheries, some of

which are in sheltered waters. Redfish, sea trout and jack crevalle inhabit the almost endless estuaries of the entire Gulf Coast and the Atlantic from Florida to the Carolinas. Snook, tarpon, bonefish, permit, barracuda, cobia and sharks are great sight-fishing challenges in the clear water of Florida. These fish of course require heavier fly tackle.

Perhaps the most widespread, available and sight-fishable inshore species of all is the redfish. Elongated barrier islands and bay estuaries form protected waters where redfish grow to maturity, feeding largely on crabs. The entire Gulf Coast from Texas to Florida, on up the east coast to South Carolina offers light-tackle sight-fishing for reds. Small craft and heavier trout gear (six- to 8+-weight) can be used to catch these fish. They hunt crabs, shrimp, mullet and other meals in water averaging 1 to 4 feet. They tail like bonefish and push humps of water as they slowly cruise for food. Though they don't jump, they fight like bulldogs. A big one can clean you out on light tackle. In some places, reds to 30-plus pounds are distinct inshore possibilities.

In most areas reds are mixed with sea trout of one to five pounds (and up to 10 pounds). These fish are aggressive feeders and keep estuary fishing interesting, but they don't have the power of other saltwater species. It's their table quality and their availability that give

An angler heads out for some shallow-water fishing in a "tricked-out" flats boat. Note the elevated platforms for enhanced fish-spotting. Less-expensive boats than this $25,000 model will get the job done in many estuaries. Skiffs, jon boats, and even canoes are used to pursue big redfish and other inshore species in protected waters along southern coasts.

them their local reputation. A freshwater trout of the same size would tow one around backwards for a week. Seatrout take poppers and streamers with equal abandon, especially in winter, when some of the glamour species are gone because of the cold.

Inshore estuaries, behind barrier islands, offer protected waters for small-boat anglers to ply. This water is mostly less than three feet deep, so big waves can't build up. Redfish love to prowl ultra-shallow flats in search of crabs, shrimp, and mullet. They'll tail like bonefish and make visible wakes to target. It's a year-round fishery in most places, though on the coldest winter days they'll drop off the flats into nearby channels and potholes where the water is a bit warmer.

Jack crevalle, relative of the illustrious permit, are another inshore fish that can put a strain on heavy trout gear. Most southern anglers look at these as trash fish, but this is strictly based on an eating-fish basis (or when one grabs a tarpon-targeted fly). Jacks are fast, strong, aggressive fighters. They terrorize baitfish schools and hunt in packs. They can often be seen churning the surface or cruising beneath it. A streamer or popper worked in front of them usually brings instant and aggressive results. They're nothing like the skittish permit in this respect. Two- to five-pound jacks will double your rod over for a good while. A 10-pounder might take 20 minutes to land. A 20-pound specimen would be unstoppable on heavy trout gear, or take 45 minutes following it around in a boat to subdue. Jacks are a true sport fish for the catch-and-release angler—numerous, aggressive and widespread.

As a general rule, small to medium redfish (one to 10 pounds) will haunt the very shallow flats much of the time. Their backs can even stick up out of the water as they prowl water as shallow as eight inches. Waking fish and "nervous water" give them away if the reds themselves can't be seen. (Some estuary waters aren't very clear.) In some areas, they distinctly favor oyster bars. As with freshwater trout, edges and dropoffs deserve an extra look or blind cast.

Seatrout, larger redfish and jacks hang out in slightly deeper flats of 2 to 5-plus feet. Grass flats pocketed with open sand patches are classic hangouts for the ambush-hunting sea trout. Pompano

This nice red was caught in two feet of water in the Indian River System around Cape Canaveral. This is one of the better areas to find big redfish in very shallow estuaries. Note the characteristic spot on the tail and blue tinge on its edge. The red's coppery color and blue-tinged tail and dorsal fin are colors to look for when sight-fishing.

Jacks are a powerful inshore (and offshore) species that terrorizes schools of baitfish. You often see them corralling baitfish at the surface, where they savagely thrash them. They take poppers and streamers aggressively, and put up long, dogged fights.

too are making a comeback on the flats, after being netted to oblivion by commercial interests (yes, eating fish has a disastrous effect on many sea and estuary environments–the "blackened redfish" craze of the 80s almost wiped reds out of many areas, till inshore net bans went into effect).

You can see where seatrout get their name. Note the yellow inside of the mouth and teeth. ("Shock tippets" of 15- to 30-pound test are preferred for most inshore species, stronger for snook and tarpon.) Seatrout fish well in winter and spring, have soft mouths and don't fight as hard as other saltwater species. Their popularity springs from their catchability and table quality. They inhabit grass flats of 2 to 6 feet in depth.

Most saltwater fish feed better on strong tidal flows, where flushing currents bring the food to them. Reds, snook, and such wait behind points, in depressions, on the downstream side of oyster bars and eat what washes by. This is obvious enough to trout anglers. In some places though, tailing and waking redfish are most visible on the lowest tides, when back bays are at their thinnest.

Most redfish have one spot on their tail, but this can vary. This "three-spotter" also sports the noticeable blue tinge along the edge of the tail fin. This shows up better than you'd think at times when spotting fish by color differences in shallow water.

This nice red took a size-2 brown crab fly. I caught him while "blind" casting in an area I had seen dozens of "tailers" the evening before. Weedless, unweighted flies are a necessity in shallow grass flats. These are usually fished very slowly for reds.

The wildlife in a rich, clear estuary is always interesting. Stingrays, crabs, shorebirds and heron are always in motion. Game fish are often sighted, even if not always caught. Porpoise cruise the deeper channels much of the day, keeping redfish chased up on the shallower flats where these top predators can't go. Some of the country's richest oyster, clam and crab-harvesting areas support great redfishing on a year-round basis.

Top redfisheries include the south and middle Texas inshore coasts (behind barrier islands). The Mississippi Delta and surrounding regions of Lousiana have some of the most prolific estuaries and backwaters around. Florida has many great redfish areas too, with additional species like snook, tarpon and barracuda mixed in along its southern reaches. The Charlotte Harbor/Pine Island South area, 10,000 Islands and the Cape Canaveral/Indian River system are among the best. Most every estuary has reds.

Redfish go for many fly patterns including Clouser's, crab patterns, "spoon flies" and poppers. Weedless size 6-1/0 hooks are preferred is most places. Chartreuse and white Clousers, brown crab patterns, bright-gold spoon flies and black flies for murky water are among the favorites. Brown and orange is another preferred color scheme, with a little bit of flash thrown in. Redfish have been known to eat anything when in the mood.

Nine- to 12-foot leaders of 8 to 15 pounds do the job. Fifteen- to 30-pound shock tippets are often added to guard against abrasion, from the fish's mouth and "crushers" (what they have in the back of their mouth to crush crabs) or from an oyster bottom. Floating lines are best in these weedy shallows. During winter cold fronts, reds seek deeper holes near the flats and migrate up estuary feeding rivers that have warmer water. A sinking line might possibly be needed.

There's no doubt about it, a southern estuary is a great place to explore when subzero weather grips the Rockies. It's not as exotic as the Pacific or Caribbean, but a small-boat-toting angler can drive

Brain Scott photo

A morning cup of tea goes down well at a New Zealand river campsite.
A long day's stalking is ahead, walking many a mile. Dreams of big fish
keep fish-stalkers going. Beautiful settings are equal rewards.
Put on the hat, daypack, and sunglasses, let's get going!

up and fish such places with conventional tackle and have some fun. (Just be sure to rinse off your equipment with fresh water each day.)

While mid winter isn't the best time, fish can still be caught. Reds, sea trout, pompano, barracuda and sharks are among the most targeted winter fisheries. Late fall is an excellent redfish time (they form big pre-spawning schools), so is from spring on (when all the other species become more active as well).

The seafood meals along these coasts are great! The smell of salt water and beautiful coastal scenes are an appealing balm for the landlocked northerner. Take your fish-stalking skills along for the ride.

Sight-fishing opportunities are endless, and always a challnge for the thinking angler. It brings you to a better understanding of your fishing environment, at home and afar. The sport becomes more interesting too. Patience in sight-fishing is vital and reaps exciting rewards. The trout's world that was once only its own, is now open to you. Look on, plan your approach, and cast true.

HATCH & FLY PATTERN CHARTS

Hatch	Fly Size	Color	Time frame	Popular Fly Patterns
Midges (Rivers & Lakes)	size 16-28	Black, Gray, tan, green-olive, red	Year round. Humid periods best. Any hours	**Dry Fly:** Griffith's Gnat, Black Midge, Parachute Midge, Adams **Wet Fly:** Midge Pupa, Palomino Midge, Midge Larva, Brassie
Little Winter Stoneflies (Rivers)	size 16-20	Black, dark brown	Late winter/ early spring. Warm afternoons	**Dry Fly:** Black Stimulator, Black Caddis, Parachute Stonefly **Wet Fly:** Montana Nymph, A.P. Black, Black Hare's Ear
Baetis Mayflies (Rivers)	size 16-20	Gray, olive-gray. nymph & spinner, rusty brown	Late March to late May (depending on elevation, etc.). Afternoons. Also Oct-Nov.	**Dry Fly:** Parachute Adams, Black Wing Baetis, Olive Sparkle Dun **Wet Fly:** Beadhead Pheasant Tail Nymph, Quigley Baetis Emerger, Standard Pheasant Tail Nymph
Western March Browns (Rivers)	size 14-16	Mottled gray-brown wing, olive-brown body	Late April/May. Late morning/early afternoon	**Dry Fly:** Parachute Adams, Brown Sparkle Dun, March Brown **Wet Fly:** Dark Hare's Ear, Standard & Beadhead
Spring Stoneflies (Rivers)	size 8-14	Black, gray-brown, olive-brown	March/May. Warm periods best. Afternoon	**Dry Fly:** Stimulator, Royal Trude **Wet Fly:** Montana Nymph, George's Stonefly Nymph, Dark Hare's Ear
Grannom Caddis (Rivers)	size 14-16	Dark gray-brown wings, olive body	Late April/early May Afternoon	**Dry Fly:** Dark Elk Hair Caddis, Partridge Caddis, Coachman Trude **Wet Fly:** Peacock & Partridge Soft Hackle
Callibaetis Mayflies (Lakes, Slow Weedy Rivers)	size 14-18	Mottled gray-tan wings and body	May/September. Late morning/ early Afternoon	**Dry Fly:** Parachute Adams, Callibaetis Dun and Spinner **Nymph:** Light Hare's Ear, Callibaetis Nymph
Large & Small Green Drake Mayflies (Rivers)	size 10-16	Veined gray wings, olive bodies	June/July (Big ones 1st, little ones a better hatch.) Late a.m./evening	**Dry Fly:** Green Drake, Paradrake, Olive Sparkle Dun **Wet Fly:** Prince Nymph, Peacock & Partridge Soft Hackle
Brown Drake (Rivers)	size 10-12	Brown mottled wings, brown-tan body	Late June/early July. Evening	**Dry Fly:** Parachute Hare's Ear, Brown Drake **Wet Fly:** Brown Drake Wiggle Nymph, Hare's Ear
Salmonfly (Rivers)	size 2-4	Gray wings, salmon-colored body highlights	Mid May/Mid July (Varies with altitude, etc.) Late AM/evening	**Dry Fly:** Stimulator, Salmonfly **Wet Fly:** Kaufmann's Stonefly Nymph, Bitch Creek, Girdle Bug
Spotted Sedge, Caddis (Rivers)	size 14-18	Mottled tan brown wings, tan body	Late May/early Nov. Afternoon/Evening.	**Dry Fly:** Elk Hair Caddis, Partridge Caddis, CDC Caddis **Wet Fly:** Hare's Ear Soft Hackle, Brown Sparkle Pupa
Golden Stonefly (Rivers)	size 4-8	Golden or tannish brown	June/early August. Morning to evening.	**Dry Fly:** Stimulator, Golden Stonefly, Madame X **Wet Fly:** Golden Stone Nymph, George's Stone, Bitch Creek, Brown Girdle Bug

HATCH & FLY PATTERN CHARTS

Hatch	Fly Size	Color	Time frame	Popular Fly Patterns
Fast-Water Mayflies (Rivers)	size 12-16	Grays, tans, pale yellows, even pink	June/October. Mid-morning to evening	**Dry Fly:** Parachute Adams, Pale Evening Dun, Light Cahill, Cream Sparkle Dun **Wet Fly:** Hare's Ear Soft Hackle, Beadhead Hare's Ear
Pale Morning Dun Mayflies (Rivers)	size 14-22	Gray-yellow wings, pale green body. Spinner pale yellow-green & rusty	Mid June/early August. Mid-morning/evening	**Dry Fly:** PMD Sparkle Dun, Parachute, PMD Spinners, CDC PMD, Light Cahill **Wet Fly:** PMD Emerger, Olive Nymph, Beadhead Pheasant Tail
Little Sister Sedge, Caddis (Rivers)	size 16-20	Mottled tan & brown wings, olive-green body	Mid-June/Mid-Sept. Morning/evening	**Dry Fly:** Elk Hair Caddis, Partridge Caddis, CDC Caddis **Wet Fly:** Peacock & Partridge Soft Hackle, Olive Sparkle Pupa
Little Yellow and Green Stoneflies (Rivers)	size 14-18	Bright green and yellows, some with red abdomens	June/early August. Mid morning/evening	**Dry Fly:** Yellow, Chartruse Humpy, Chartreuse Trude, Parachute PMD **Wet Fly:** Mini Golden Stone Nymph, Brown & Yellow Montana Nymph
Trico Mayfly (Rivers and Lakes)	size 18-24	Light gray-clear wings. Olive-black body	Early July/Mid-Sept. Mornings	**Dry Fly:** Olive Sparkle Dun, Parachute Trico, CDC Trico, Trico Spinner **Wet Fly:** Not Generally Imitated
Traveler Sedge, Caddis (Lakes)	size 6-10	Tannish brown	May/July (Couple weeks after ice goes off.) Whenever seen	**Dry Fly:** Elk Hair Caddis, Stimulator (skid and twitched across surface) **Wet Fly:** Hare's Ear Soft Hackle
Tiny Blue-Winged Olive (Rivers)	size 22-26	Light gray wings, green to tan body	July/Sept. Afternoon/evening	**Dry Fly:** Green Sparkle Dun, Parachute Olive, Olive Thorax, CDC Olive **Wet Fly:** Pheasant Tail Nymph, Olive Emerger
Small Western Red Quill (Rivers)	size 14-16	Reddish brown	July/early September. Late morning. Spinners, dusk	**Dry Fly:** Parachute Pheasant Tail, Brown Hairwing Dun **Wet Fly:** Dark Hare's Ear, Soft Hackle
Mahogany Dun (Rivers)	size 16	Gray wings, reddish-brown body	September/early November. Late morning/afternoon	**Dry Fly:** Mahogany Dun, Parachute Pheasant Tail **Wet Fly:** Pheasant Tail Nymph, Dark Hare's Ear
Baetis Mayflies (Rivers)	size 16-20	See above	See above	See "Beatis Mayflies," page 62
October Caddis (Rivers)	size 6-8	Gray wings, dirty-orange body	Late September/early November Late morning/evening	**Dry Fly:** Stimulator, Goddard October Caddis, Bucktail Caddis **Wet Fly:** Orange Woolly Worm, October Caddis, Sparkle Pupa
Midges (Rivers and Lakes)	size 16-28	See above	See above	See "Midges," page 62

Notes on the Fly Chart

There are many other hatches besides those listed, of varying regional importance. Some, like the black caddis and pale evening dun for instance, are very important on some waters, yet nonexistent on others. Hatch dates can vary greatly too, affected by altitude, coastal weather influences, and because of a dam's effect on water temperatures. Cloudy, drizzly weather will often extend a hatch's hours from what it would be on a hot sunny day. Morning and evening hatches can both pop on rainy afternoons, when many overlapping hatches could be seen.

As far as steadily rising fish go, midges, mayflies, and caddis bring up the most. size 16-26 midge patterns in black, gray, olive, tan, and red cover most bases. Lake midges run larger than river midges. Larva, pupa, emerger, and adult patterns are all important.

The most prolific mayfly species are size 14-24s. Body colors to have on hand include olive, green, brown, tan, cream and gray. Rusty browns are common spent-wing colors, which also include cream, pale yellow/green, tan and black. Pink and orange hued grays are colors that work well too at times. Grayish wings are most common among the freshly hatched mayflies or "duns." These tend to be darker in spring and fall hatching flies, and lighter in the summer species. The spent-wing or dying egg-layers have glassy, clear wings. Most mayfly body colors change a bit when they molt to the egg-laying stage or "spinner." Males and females often have different colors as well. With some mayfly species, PMDs for example, "emergers" can be of great importance. This varies from hatch to hatch.

The most prolific caddis come in size 14-20s. Medium or cinnamon brown bodies are most common, with mottled brown wings. Olive to Granny Smith apple green come in second, with gray or brown mottled wings. There are many variations, from black to almost white. Caddis can be as big as size 6, and as small as size 26. Medium or cinnamon brown flies in size16-18 account for most of my action. There are many cases when more realistic imitations are better than bushy Elk Hair Caddis types. This is especially true on flat water. Caddis emergers play a big role in most locales as well. I often fish one as a dropper off a high-floating caddis dry.

A little inquiry can go a long way in improving your catch rate. Check with local experts for important hatch tips, whether it's a fly shop owner, guide or fly club member. Specific hatch hours, locally effective patterns and specialized techniques are all of interest. Most accomplished fly fishermen will be happy to give you some pointers.

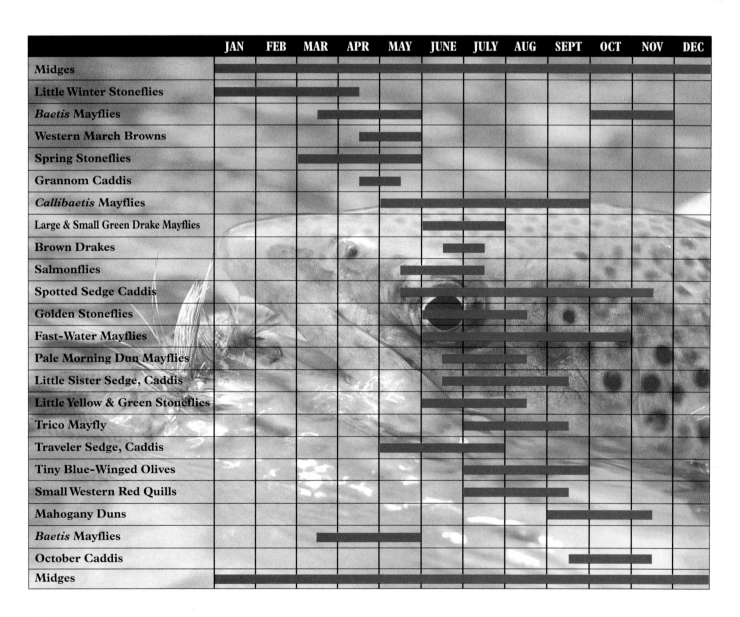

	JAN	FEB	MAR	APR	MAY	JUNE	JULY	AUG	SEPT	OCT	NOV	DEC
Midges	■	■	■	■	■	■	■	■	■	■	■	■
Little Winter Stoneflies	■	■	■	■								
Baetis Mayflies			■	■	■					■	■	
Western March Browns				■	■							
Spring Stoneflies			■	■	■							
Grannom Caddis				■	■							
Callibaetis Mayflies					■	■	■	■	■			
Large & Small Green Drake Mayflies						■	■					
Brown Drakes						■						
Salmonflies					■	■	■					
Spotted Sedge Caddis					■	■	■	■	■	■		
Golden Stoneflies						■	■	■				
Fast-Water Mayflies					■	■	■	■	■	■		
Pale Morning Dun Mayflies						■	■	■	■			
Little Sister Sedge, Caddis						■	■	■				
Little Yellow & Green Stoneflies						■	■	■				
Trico Mayfly							■	■	■			
Traveler Sedge, Caddis					■	■	■					
Tiny Blue-Winged Olives							■	■	■	■		
Small Western Red Quills							■	■	■	■		
Mahogany Duns									■	■	■	
Baetis Mayflies			■	■	■							
October Caddis										■	■	
Midges	■	■	■	■	■	■	■	■	■	■	■	■